POLITICAL
LANGUAGE
Words That Succeed
and Policies That Fail

This is a volume in the

Institute for Research on Poverty Monograph Series

A complete list of titles in this series appears at the end of this volume.

POLITICAL LANGUAGE
Words That Succeed and Policies That Fail

MURRAY EDELMAN

Department of Political Science and
Institute for Research on Poverty
University of Wisconsin—Madison
Madison, Wisconsin

With an Introduction by
Michael Lipsky

Academic Press   NEW YORK   SAN FRANCISCO   LONDON
A Subsidiary of Harcourt Brace Jovanovich, Publishers

This book is one of a series sponsored by the Institute for Research on Poverty of the University of Wisconsin pursuant to the provisions of the Economic Opportunity Act of 1964.

ACADEMIC PRESS, INC.
111 Fifth Avenue, New York, New York 10003

United Kingdom Edition published by
ACADEMIC PRESS, INC. (LONDON) LTD.
24/28 Oval Road, London NW1

Library of Congress Cataloging in Publication Data

Edelman, Jacob Murray,   Date
      Political language.

      (Institute for Research on Poverty monograph series)
      Includes bibliographical references and index.
      1.   Sociolinguistics.   2.   Political psychology.
3.   United States—Social conditions.   I.   Title.
II.   Series: Wisconsin.   University—Madison.
Institute for Research on Poverty.   Monograph series.
HM291.E3   320'.01'4   76-52710
ISBN 0–12–230660–0 (cloth)
ISBN 0–12–230662–7 (paper)

PRINTED IN THE UNITED STATES OF AMERICA

81 82   9 8 7 6 5 4 3

To the memory of
Kalman and Sadie Edelman

Contents

Foreword

In *Political Language: Words That Succeed and Policies That Fail,*
Murray Edelman attempts to "explain the acceptance of large and
chronic inequalities that give the most of what there is to get to a
small proportion of the population." As he notes, many social scientists and the public at large appear to take the existence of such inequality for granted. More attention is devoted to explaining political
challenges to poverty and inequality than to explaining the acceptance
of poverty and inequality. Why is this so? Why do the poorer members of society accept their relatively small share?

Edelman's stimulating and controversial hypothesis is that language and symbols create problematic beliefs in both elites and nonelites that facilitate the quiescent acceptance of chronic poverty and
inequality. For example, he argues that public bureaucracies are more
effective in using language to shape beliefs about what they do than
they are in dealing with the chronic social problems that they are
supposed to ameliorate. Similarly, he argues that "The helping professions are the most effective contemporary agents of social conformity and isolation . . . yet are largely spared from self-criticism,

from political criticism, and even from political observation through a special symbolic language."

Although the question of why poverty and substantial inequalities persist in a democratic society has been pursued by other political scientists and economists, Murray Edelman is the first researcher at the Institute for Research on Poverty who has attempted to explore it. This analysis of the importance of language as symbol builds upon his previously published Institute monograph *Politics as Symbolic Action*

Political Language: Words That Succeed and Policies That Fail is an important contribution and should be studied by anyone seriously interested in the politics of inequality.

> *Irwin Garfinkel*
> Director, Institute for
> Research on Poverty

Acknowledgments

As the first to discuss these issues with me, my students deserve, and have, my gratitude. Anticipation of their reactions forced me to think and helped me avoid pitfalls; and when anticipation was not enough, they often made me discard material that would have weakened or confused my argument.

I am also grateful to the friends and colleagues who have commented on the manuscript, especially Charles Anderson, Lloyd Etheredge, Kenneth Farmer, Booth Fowler, Joseph Gusfield, Michael Lipsky, Anne Machung, Richard Merelman, Linda Burzotta Nilson, and Rozann Rothman. Needless to say, these readers often questioned my presentation and doubtless still disapprove of some of it, though they helped immeasurably to improve the book.

Parts of Chapters 1 and 2 are revisions of an article that appeared in *Society* 12 (July–August 1975): 14–21. Chapter 4 appeared as an article in *Politics and Society* 4 (Fall 1974): 295–310. A part of Chapter 8 appeared in *The Progressive* 39 (May 1975).

The research was supported in part by the Institute for Research on Poverty, a Senior Fellowship from the National Endowment for the Humanities, and a supplemental grant from the Graduate College of the University of Wisconsin—Madison. I am grateful to the Sociology Department of the London School of Economics for providing me an office and a stimulating intellectual atmosphere during part of the time I was writing this book.

M.E.

Introduction

When the mind's eye has grown accustomed to the view that American society is scarred with persistent inequalities, injustice, and above all marked discrepancies between promise and performance, the task becomes the explanation of the relative passivity of the victims. How is it that people accept poverty amid affluence, hopelessness in a land of opportunity, government by unresponsive institutions that are pledged to human service? Why do they not rebel or at least speak out more forcefully against the political and social order?

The irony of American politics is that it rests on the "consent" of the governed. I mean this not in the conventional sense that leaders are responsible to an electorate, or that laws depend upon their continued acceptability. Rather, "consent of the governed" currently means popular acquiescence to political and economic structures and relationships in which many people do not thrive, are trapped, and exercise little independent initiative. Perspectives that challenge the status quo are not accorded the legitimacy that would make them subjects of serious discussion; untrustworthy politicians are accorded trust; political discourse is trivialized and ritualized.

Any complex social reality is likely to be open to a variety of interpretations. One might argue, for example, that people characteristically do dissent from the status quo, that the "consent of the governed" only captures a portion of the reality. Or one might draw upon a pluralist analysis of American politics to suggest that the openness of the political system diverts dissent into acceptable and normal political activities. But neither acknowledging the American tradition of protest and dissent nor conceptualizing American politics as essentially pluralistic detracts from these observations. It is true that American politics has always entertained protest and dissent, but most people do not overtly support protest movements, even when those movements purport to act in their interests, and those who do generally have not been able to sustain participation once initial objectives have been achieved or their movement has encountered significant obstacles. Protest movements simultaneously offer the best hope for transforming American politics, yet, instructively, tend to be difficult to sustain.

The pluralistic aspects of American politics, through opportunities for individual, direct participation in politics and through group affiliations, might seem at first glance to provide people with the chance to affect political life. Yet careful analysis of pluralist assumptions over the past ten years reveals that pluralism does not substantially contradict the proposition that American politics manipulates mass attitudes and perspectives. Pluralism may ensure competition among elites and at times may provide masses with opportunities to participate in decision making, thus conveying a sense that popular democracy thrives. But pluralism in practice also means elite dominion on the major issues salient to elites, severe limitations on protest group activity, and manipulation of the terms on which "issues" arise and are processed.

Writing at this date, midway through the 1970s and just before the presidential election, the striking facts about mass participation in America are these. Vigorous mass dissent is not apparent, although economic conditions are generally as severe as they have been in a generation. And inclinations to participate in conventional politics— with projections for turnout in November hovering at a historically low 50 percent level—are also conspicuously low.

The pluralist tradition scarcely prepares us for these developments. To a pluralist analyst, low participation may be explained either as mass satisfaction or by an elite theory—not necessarily incompatible

—that comments negatively on the inherently low interest of people in politics. The analyst of dissent who rejects these perspectives must explain the normally low participation in protest as either despair over the likelihood of success or as suppression. Confounding these perspectives in one way or another is the general observation that the political system is relatively open to participation. If it is relatively open, then surely what must be explained is the failure to take advantage of opportunities.

Those who study conventional political activity, and those who study emergent protest politics, have often approached their subjects as if they were analytic antagonists. However, although analyses of pluralism and protest often vary considerably in their perspectives and orientations, they have shared a commitment to studying manifest political behaviors. That is, they have been committed to studying political activity that is (readily) observable. Thus pluralists, observing a degree of participation in politics, see signs of health. Thus students of dissent, analyzing the tendency of ordinary people to transcend conventional political channels, see signs of vigor in the willingness of some people to protest, and signs of conservatism in the capacity of elites to contain protest activity. But both protest and pluralist analysis direct attention to overt *activity*, when the more interesting and certainly more critical political observation is that most people generally neither protest nor participate to any great degree.

Many students of American politics have been chronically unable to analyze the characteristically low levels of participation and dissent successfully because they have trained themselves to focus attention exclusively on what they call behavior, by which they mean readily observable actions. Thus survey research, roll calls, and various interviewing techniques have thrived as bases for analysis because they display actions (or surrogates for actions) or provide insight into attitudes, the motivational background for actions. The difficulty with research of this kind is that there is a range of political developments to which the researcher is blind. This is the area of *caused inaction*, inaction best explained as induced by influences outside of the individual. The fawn, unmoving in the thicket, may be asleep, but it also may be paralyzed with fear of a predator. In the latter case, only the observer who is alert to the structure of power will provide a persuasive account of the fawn's behavior.

One alternative to the obvious inadequacies of an orthodox behaviorist perspective is to focus on the relative power and status of different groups in the society and to proceed from the assumption that dominant groups are in conflict with subordinate groups and will seek to maintain their dominant position, particularly in matters of importance to them. From this perspective dominant groups will seek to minimize concessions to subordinate groups. This perspective is consistent with observations that minimal concessions tend to result from vigorous popular protest and that new political groups (such as labor unions) tend to be incorporated into the constellations of power strictly on terms that do not require fundamentally new arrangements. Yet it is not a static perspective. Important changes, when they do occur, may be explained by the implicit choice of elites that it will be less costly to make concessions than to resist them and that they will be able to manage the terms of concessions to their advantage.

While this perspective on politics is promising, it is somewhat sterile unless one begins to explicate the *mechanisms* by which elites maintain advantage over nonelites. It is not enough to say that some groups have power, others do not, and that these relationships are fairly stable. For this view to be persuasive it is necessary to demonstrate that this stability, this structuring of power, is itself dynamic; that this stability is not simply a social fact but a social *process*. Moreover, this social process is not dominated by coercion—although coercion is always in the background when authority is the basis of relationships. Thus, we return to our first question: how is the "consent of the governed" obtained in the society when there are great disparities in wealth, status, and power, and strong presumptions that groups enjoying little of these would profit from a change in their relationship to the rest of society?

For people seeking to address these concerns Murray Edelman has guided the way. Beginning with *The Symbolic Uses of Politics* (1964) he has shown how, in communications between political authorities and mass publics, elites significantly structure the expectations people have of them and significantly contribute to the accepting relationship of mass publics to authority itself. He has demonstrated a subtle way of analyzing the public pronouncements and actions of authorities in terms of their symbolic content and their psychological impact on a dependent population seeking reassurance and virtually demanding leadership. He has argued persuasively that the reverence for an autonomous "public opinion" is misplaced, since leaders themselves tend to cue mass publics to hold perceptions to which they later "respond."

He has gone beyond recognizing that public policies often do not result in actions consistent with the stated intentions of the framers. Rather, as in the case of regulatory commissions, he has made a convincing case for the view that the material impact of policy is likely to favor dominant groups while the symbolic aspects of the policy falsely reassure mass publics that their interests are protected against the rapaciousness of powerful groups.

In *Politics as Symbolic Action* (1971), an inquiry that began during the ghetto riots of the mid-1960s and gained vigor during the mass demonstrations against the war in Indochina, Edelman continued his investigations into the symbolic dimensions of politics, but here concentrated as much on symbolic interactions that contribute both to mass mobilization and the escalation of conflict as well as to mass passivity. Throughout, he has drawn attention to the problematic nature of social "facts" and those aspects of mass psychology for which political pronouncements answer underlying needs. Thus elite pronouncements feed into and partially create the language structures in terms of which people understand the world and psychologically defend their place in the world from contradiction. From this perspective, politics does not begin with mass emotion or policy preferences but with conceptual structures into which people receive information and transform it into a world view from which action (or inaction) proceeds.

Murray Edelman has provided a powerful analytical framework to understand the "consent" of the governed. He has shown how relationships of power are manifested in daily life through language forms, myths, and symbolic responses to profound public needs for reassurance and order. *Political Language: Words That Succeed and Policies That Fail* provides a different approach to this developing perspective. Here he focuses on the processing of conceptions of poverty and other "needs" by mass publics, experts and professionals charged with dealing with poor or dependent people, and people who are poor or otherwise dependent. While in other works he dealt with such generic behavioral phenomena as mass arousal and quiescence, in this volume he focuses on the meaning of public policy through disciplined attention to conceptions of poverty and social welfare. Thus we see more clearly than before how ubiquitous, subtle, and virtually unobtrusive are the contributions of elites and masses alike to the maintenance of the status quo. If previous works tended to focus on pronouncements of policy and well-reported, newsworthy events, such as riots or international crises, this book draws attention to the political implications of commonplace, routine language. This, too, contributes to an evolving understanding of the contributions of elites and masses to the low-level, continuous management of conflict on terms that restrict the opportunities perceived and seized by subordinate groups. The analysis also gives prominence to the mediating roles of organized professionals and bureaucracies controlling the relationship between people and the agencies that often have power over them.

It is hazardous to venture introductory remarks to Murray Edelman's work. A brief commentary cannot convey the richness of his analysis or begin to discuss his control of the eclectic mix of scholarly sources on which his complex arguments are based. Nor can it adequately communicate the modesty of the presentation; Edelman seems to write as if he feels he has slightly less to say than first appearances might indicate. Indeed, it is perhaps for this reason that an introduction is warranted at all. Murray Edelman's work has encouraged a generation of students of American politics to develop perspectives outside of the mainstream of democratic mythology. Yet he has been disinclined to elaborate fully on the implications of his work. Others (and he himself) might wish to emphasize different aspects of *Political Language: Words That Succeed and Policies That Fail* than the ones stressed here. But those who have followed his work will agree that it is central to a developing and increasingly vigorous effort to see clearly the subtle aspects of social control that pervade our relationships and induce popular consent to the political order.

Michael Lipsky
Cambridge, Massachusetts
October, 1976

Chronic Problems,
Banal Language, and
Contradictory Beliefs

The Acceptance of Inequality

Gross differences in the quality of people's lives, in personal autonomy, in power, and in dignity have always marked the human condition. In contemporary industrialized societies, inequalities remain large and are closely linked to the controversial issues with which governments deal, most clearly to the social problems that are never solved: poverty, crime, and inability to adapt to the life one has to lead. Inequality in income and in wealth has been substantial in America since the seventeenth century; its persistence and stability are more striking than occasional fluctuations.[1] Even during the sustained effort to help the poor that was called a "war on poverty"

Parts of this chapter are revisions of Murray Edelman, "Language and Social Problems," *Society* 12 (July–August 1975): 14–21. © 1975 Transaction, Inc.
[1] See Peter H. Lindert and Jeffrey G. Williamson, "Three Centuries of American Inequality," University of Wisconsin—Madison, Institute for Research on Poverty, Discussion Paper 333–76; Willford I. King, *Wealth and Income of the People of the United States* (New York: Macmillan, 1915); Herman P. Miller,

in the 1960s, the poorest did not improve their condition in comparison with the general standard of living.[2] In 1976 the Secretary-General of the United Nations reported that there were a larger number of impoverished people in the world than ever before, after a century of misdirected technological progress and of an accumulation of social problems that were due primarily to ineffective social organization and policies.[3]

Can we explain the acceptance of large and chronic inequalities that give the most of what there is to get to a small proportion of the population who, by and large, acquire disproportionate influence and status as well as disproportionate wealth? Does the acceptance of inequality even need explanation? We commonly take inequality for granted while regarding mass challenges to it as a "phenomenon" calling for inquiry.[4] I focus here upon language and symbols that justify acceptance of inequality and tolerance of chronic social problems. The quiescent acceptance of chronic inequality, deprivation, and daily indignities is surely revealing, occurring as it does in a society in which we teach children, and repeat frequently to adults as well, that people are created equal, that this is a land of equal opportunity, and that democracy means respect for the dignity of the individual.

Banality and Anxiety

Poverty is chronic and universal, and the political language in which its causes, consequences, victims, and remedies are most widely

---

Income Distribution in the United States, 1960 Census Monograph (Washington, D.C.: U.S. Government Printing Office, 1966), p. 20.

The concentration of wealth in America dropped during the 1930s and 1940s, but it has been increasing somewhat since the 1950s. A leading study estimated that the top 1 percent held 26 percent of the national wealth in 1956; the figure is very likely higher in the 1970s. See Robert J. Lampman, *The Share of the Top Wealth-Holders in National Wealth* (Princeton: Princeton University Press, 1962), p. 24.

[2] See Robert D. Plotnick and Felicity Skidmore, *Progress against Poverty: A Review of the 1964–1974 Decade* (New York: Academic Press, 1975), pp. 104–5, 169–79.

[3] *New York Times,* 1 June 1976, p. 4.

[4] For a persuasive discussion of the sense in which scientific inquiry is shaped by what is regarded as part of the natural order or, alternatively, singled out as

discussed is as predictable as the problem itself. Chronic social problems, recurring beliefs about them, and recurring language forms that
justify their acceptance reinforce each other. Only rarely can there
be direct observations of events, and even then language forms shape
the meaning of what the general public and government officials
see. It is language that evokes most of the political "realities" people
experience. The challenge is to learn how language and gestures are
systematically transformed into complex cognitive structures.

My major concern is with banality in the language and acts with
which governments deal with chronic social problems, with the beliefs it generates, and with the consequences for politics and society.
Linguistic forms, public actions, and reactions to them that recur in
everyday life are my data.

In politics, as in religion, whatever is ceremonial or banal strengthens reassuring beliefs regardless of their validity and discourages
skeptical inquiry about disturbing issues. From the beginnings of recorded history to the present day, governments have won the support of large numbers of their citizens for policies that were based
upon delusions: beliefs in witches, in nonexistent internal and external enemies, or in the efficacy of laws to regulate private power,
cope with destitution, guarantee civil rights, or rehabilitate criminals
that have often had the opposite effect from their intended ones.
Large numbers of people continue for long periods of time to cling
to myth,[5] to justify it in formulas that are repeated in their cultures,
and to reject falsifying information when prevailing myths justify
their interests, roles, and past actions, or assuage their fears.

Understandably, beliefs differ as people's interests and their social
situations do. Some see ghetto riots as signifying the wretchedness
of the black poor; others see them as evidence of subversion by outside agitators; and still others see them as proof of the psychopathol-
ogy of the rioters. Here again, the same facts admit a range of
meanings. Problematic beliefs are especially likely to arise in ambiguous situations that engender anxiety.

Consider the sense in which political language and actions reflect

---

a "phenomenon," see Stephen Toulmin, *Foresight and Understanding* (New York:
Harper and Row, 1961).

[5] A "myth" is not necessarily a fiction. The term signifies a widely accepted
belief that gives meaning to events and that is socially cued, whether or not it is
verifiable.

uncertainty, insecurity, and threat, and engender problematic beliefs about ambiguous events. Knowing they are often helpless to control their own fate, people resort to religion and to government to cope with anxieties they cannot otherwise ward off. We want to be re-assured that "Man is the captain of his fate" because we know that he or she too often is not: that whether people live a happy or a miserable life, what work they do, their level of self-respect, the status they achieve, and the time they die depend heavily on condi-tions over which they have little control. Government presents itself as protector against a gamut of dangers ranging from foreign military attack through criminal attack and food shortages to un-employment, poverty, and sickness.

Like religion, politics both arouses and assuages anxiety, though people typically think of government as a rational device for achiev-ing their wants and see their own political opinions and actions as the epitome of reasoned behavior. Families and public schools rein-force this optimistic view in small children.[6] Yet, governments shape many public beliefs and demands before they respond to the people's will.[7] Eagerness to believe that government will ward off evils and threats renders us susceptible to political language that both intensi-fies and eases anxiety at least as powerfully as the language of religion does. The Defense Department tells Americans repeatedly both that Russia is surpassing us in one or another form of weapon system and that American armed forces are prepared to defend the country. The FBI tells us repeatedly both that crime is increasing and that the FBI has never been more effective in coping with it.

If political language both excites and mollifies fears, language is an integral facet of the political scene: not simply an instrument for describing events but itself a part of events, shaping their meaning and helping to shape the political roles officials and the general pub-lic play. In this sense, language, events, and self-conceptions are a part of the same transaction, mutually determining one another's meanings.

"Security" is very likely the primal political symbol, for threats

[6] David Easton and Jack Dennis, *Children in the Political System* (New York: McGraw-Hill, 1969); Fred I. Greenstein, *Children and Politics*, rev. ed. (New Haven: Yale University Press, 1968).

[7] I discuss and document this proposition in Murray Edelman, *The Symbolic Uses of Politics* (Urbana: University of Illinois Press, 1964); and Murray Edel-man, *Politics as Symbolic Action* (New York: Academic Press, 1971).

engage people intensely in news of public affairs. Through the evocation of threat and reassurance, leaders gain followings and people are induced to accept sacrifices and to remain susceptible to appeals for support. The willingness of mass publics to follow, to sacrifice, to accept their roles is the basic necessity for every political regime. Without a following there are no leaders. For governments and for aspirants to leadership it is therefore important both that people become anxious about their security and that their anxiety be assuaged, though never completely so. "National security," "social security," and similar terms are potent symbols, though synonyms for them are sometimes necessary to avoid banality.

Obviously, there are perceptions of social problems based on observations and analyses that are relatively uninfluenced by social pressures. Such analyses do not echo recurring formulas, but they are seldom the chief influences upon public policy toward problems like poverty. Stylized language forms and cognitions make it hard for the careful formulations to win political acceptance.

Social Adjustment through Contradictory Beliefs

In every culture people learn to explain chronic problems through alternative sets of assumptions that are inconsistent with one another; yet the contradictory formulas persist, rationalizing inconsistent public policies and inconsistent individual beliefs about the threats that are widely feared in everyday life. The pervasiveness of such contradictory myths is apparent enough, but their role in shaping public opinion and political support is not. The work of structural anthropologists and linguists on cultural contradictions suggests a way of analyzing the political functions of contradictory beliefs that are never resolved.

Consider some examples of persisting but contradictory cognitions regarding common social problems. Poverty and the dependency that goes with it are ubiquitous through history and in every country. Workers in the factories of early nineteenth-century England, residents of the ghettos of American cities today, French mine workers in the nineteenth century, Indian peasants, and children everywhere exemplify people dependent for their subsistence upon others and never sure to get it. In these and thousands of similar cases, historical accounts, like contemporary experience, reveal that the most common cognitive reactions to poverty fall into a small set of forms that are classic, predictable, ritualistic, and banal.

One pattern defines the poor as responsible for their own plight and in need of control to compensate for their inadequacies, greed, lack of self-discipline, immorality, pathology, or criminal tendencies, while authorities, including concerned professionals, cope more or less competently with the deviant and protect a basically sound social structure from the threat they pose. Officials and economic elites responsible for keeping others dependent lean toward this view. It appears in the statements of English factory owners in the nineteenth century and in similar pronouncements of American industrialists after the growth of a factory economy in the United States. It is a recurrent litany of legislators, judges, and administrators who oppose increases in welfare benefits and in minimum wages, and who want to curb union power. It is also a theme of conventional psychiatrists and social workers, expressed in their case in the professional language of mental illness, help, reinforcement, delinquency, and rehabilitation.[8] This view justifies regulation of the poor, while leaving it unclear in what sense governmental and professional interventions are social control and in what sense they are "rehabilitation." Call this pattern one.

An alternative recurring reaction to poverty defines the poor as victims of exploitative economic, social, and political institutions: people deprived by circumstances (not by their personal defects) and likely to become immoral and dangerous unless they are allowed to fulfill their potentialities, while authorities and helping professionals serve the interests of other elite groups. Liberal and leftist politicians, many sociologists, and helping professionals who dissent from the conventional ideology of their professions lean toward this view. Call it pattern two.

Though each person's social situation is likely to make one or the other of these perspectives his or her dominant one, everybody learns both of them, for they are stock explanations of a universal phenomenon. The poor and the affluent, like everyone else, learn to perceive poverty in both ways and to emphasize one or the other view as necessary to justify their roles, to account for developments

[8] See Chapter 4.

in the news, and to adjust to changing social situations. In this sense both perspectives are part of the culture, enabling people to live with themselves and with practices that would otherwise bring guilt and continuous social upheaval.

To embrace pattern two when confronted with stark suffering or blatant mistreatment of poor people while embracing pattern one to justify avoidance of active protest and general support of prevailing institutions is a common response; but the availability of both views makes possible a wide spectrum of ambivalent postures for each individual and a similarly large set of contradictions in political rhetoric and in public policy. Both patterns of belief are present in our culture and in our minds, ready to serve our egos when we need them. Because the problem persists, it must be resolved through language and through governmental actions. The rhetorical embrace of one stylized belief may reflect qualms about acceptance of the other in one's work or politics. The coexistence of contradictory reactions to a "problem" from which many benefit helps assure that it will be deplored but tolerated, rather than attacked in a resolute way.

Neither stock explanation has any necessary bearing on the "facts." Either may in some sense be valid. But validity is neither a help nor a hindrance to the employment of these explanations as rationalizations for individual beliefs and public policies. They persist regardless of the causes of inequality and poverty, which remain problematic and controversial. Because individual competence or inadequacy doubtless depends upon subtle links among social conditions and biological balances that vary with the individual and are little understood, there is always "evidence" of a sort for either view; and because both explanations depend upon unprovable premises about society and the individual, the observer's values and interests play the crucial part in the acceptance of one or the other view.

Quiescent public acceptance of poverty as a fact of social life depends upon how it is defined, far more than upon its severity. To define it, and therefore perceive it, in terms of the inherent inadequacies of the poor person is to treat its symptoms in individuals, usually in ways that ensure high rates of recidivism, whether the treatment consists of welfare benefits, imprisonment for crime, or hospitalization for emotional disturbance. Those who define it in terms of the functioning of the economic system are, in my view, dealing with causes rather than symptoms. But their categories also encourage continued acceptance of poverty as a "problem"; for terms like "system" and "economic law" make poverty look either unconquerable or so hard to change that few will support the political effort. Both human "nature" and social "system" are categories that engender acceptance of things as they are and of problems as chronic. This is a discouraging view, but an optimistic one would hardly fit the historical record.

We find, then, a pair of opposing political myths for each of the conflicting cognitive patterns that define our attitudes toward social problems, the authorities who deal with them, and the people who suffer from them. Ambivalence is reflected in concomitant myths, each of them internally consistent, though they are inconsistent with each other. At the same time the availability in the culture of the opposing belief permits the individual to reconcile contradictions and live with his or her ambivalence.[9]

The parts of a structure of cognitions evoke, reinforce, and transform into each other. To believe that the poor are responsible for their poverty is to exonerate economic and political institutions from that responsibility and to legitimize the efforts of authorities to change the poor person's attitudes and behavior. Each of these beliefs implies the others in the cognitive structure, even though we conventionally experience them as three distinct beliefs about (1) the psychology of the poor, (2) the roles of authorities, and (3) the health of the economy and the polity. A reference to any part of the structure evokes the entire structure. This cognitive structure justifies the status, power, and roles of the middle class, public officials, and helping professionals, and provides an acceptable reason to maintain inequalities, though it does so ambivalently. A large part of the working class and the poor also have reason to accept this pattern of belief, for they have little ground for self-esteem except their identification with the state and the elite. This belief pattern is therefore the dominant one. I am concerned here with how beliefs come to be evoked and with their consequences, not with their tenability.

---

[9] Claude Lévi-Strauss suggests that folk myths incorporate "unwelcome contradictions"; and his insight clarifies the function of contemporary myths about social problems as well. According to Lévi-Strauss, "The purpose of myth is to provide a logical model capable of overcoming a contradiction (an impossible achievement if, as it happens, the contradiction is real)." Claude Lévi-Strauss, *Structural Anthropology* (New York: Basic Books, 1963), p. 229.

Symbolic Evocation and Political Reality

What is appearance and what is reality? The analysis of changing, conflicting, and problematic perceptions raises that classic question with special insistence. That the issue *is* classic means that it has not been resolved and very likely that it cannot be.

One premise is clear enough: public policies rest on the beliefs and perceptions of those who help make them, whether or not those cognitions are accurate. People executed as witches in the seventeenth century and those persecuted in witch hunts in the twentieth century suffered from the definitions applied to them regardless of the correctness of either form of belief in witches. The analyst of public policy formation needs to know how cognitions are evoked and how they are structured, whether or not they are "realistic" in any sense.

The tenability of these beliefs depends at least in part on what people take for granted and on what they value as they experience political phenomena. In that sense *political* cognitions would seem to have a rather different epistemological status from the knowledge of the hard sciences, contrary to the view that the methods of inquiry of the natural sciences are an ideal that social scientists should emulate. For those who accept the latter position, the challenge for a social scientist is to gather and organize pertinent observations and to verify or falsify the propositions they suggest. Observations of political events can be adequately objective and consensual. The important question is how often particular cognitions and behaviors occur. The answers describe what is real, and the social scientist's job is to discover it.

Such research reflects the prevailing cognitions of respondents and researchers and, therefore, the dominant contemporary ideology; for it reproduces whatever people have been socialized to perceive and believe, rather than analyzing the range of alternative symbolic evocations. However many physicists read a thermometer or measure the volume of liquid in a beaker, their observations are normally close—not because the observer's interests are irrelevant to what he or she perceives but because the norms of professional physics define the observer's paramount interest when he is making such observations; so that physicists make essentially the same assumptions regarding which properties of the observed objects are relevant, the meanings of those properties, and the functions of their instruments for observation.

The involvement of a social scientist with the most persistent political issues (inequality, poverty, economic insecurity, war, unconventional behavior, rebellion) is drastically different, though the difference is not typically self-conscious and a posture of scientism may mask it. The perception of such political issues resonates with observers' fears, hopes, and interests and with the roles they play. How political events are perceived defines the observer as surely as he or she defines them. To see a prisoner convicted of assault either as a psychopath or as a victim of poverty is to identify one's own psychological and political posture at least as firmly as one identifies that of the prisoner.

But we easily accept both views as we change settings and roles or acquire new information. Because our lives entail conflicting concerns respecting controversial contemporary issues, political cognitions are likely to be complex and internally contradictory, while taking account of the same "facts." Political beliefs and perceptions remain partly enigma, continuously threatening and reassuring, changing in appearance, knowable only in terms of what is systematic about their changes.

There is no one "real" perception, then, but a cognitive structure with alternative facets, possibilities, and combinations appearing as the observer encounters new situations. To take a response to the simple stimulus offered by a survey interviewer or experimenter as *the* factual cognition of the respondent is to impoverish the research, the minds of observers, and the minds of everyone engaged with political issues. The very word "respondent" is an impoverishment: the cue to a language game that erases from the world most of what people think, feel, and do about an issue and *all* of what they might think, feel, and do in different situations. Survey researchers contribute to such an impoverishment only if they assume, or create the impression in others, that the only model of reality is the one their particular choice of observational instruments and assumptions produces.

Conventional social science defines observations as "empirical" very largely when they are made in artificial social situations that are frequently created by the researcher himself: a respondent being interviewed as part of a research project, for example, or a student induced to take part in an experiment. Such "empiricism" eliminates the everyday context of multiple and shifting cues; that is the purpose of the artificiality. To the positivist, research is most gratifyingly "empirical" when it defines the *researcher's* phenomena as "fact," while avoiding observation of the wide range of relevant phenomena in people's everyday political worlds.

The most persistent and controversial political issues, then, *are* the complex cognitive structures people acquire about them. A cubist painting is a metaphor for their "reality," for they reflect perceptions that are multifaceted and internally contradictory, changing with the vantage point of the observer. To explain does not involve discovery of what has previously been unknown but a strategy for dealing with complexity and subtlety.

Cognitions are complex because they are social in character, not confined inside the head of a single person. Language and gestures generate shared meanings at the same time as they generate a "self," though recognition of the social basis of individual cognition in no way denies individuality. Class ties, group identifications, reference groups, and other kinds of "significant others" help shape patterns of belief, but every individual differs in some degree from any other in the pattern of his or her role-taking.

Yet everyone must have some sensitivity to conflicting identifications, as my earlier references to contradictory cognitions suggest. The psychiatrist who defines a welfare recipient who failed to report all her assets as a "sociopath" and the policeman who perceives every lawbreaker in the slum as inherently evil both know that the behavior they label as individual pathology is also a response to poverty, dependency, and economic conditions. But the policeman and the psychiatrist, like everyone else, are likely to focus on definitions of people and situations that call for the skills and authority they have, rather than those others have; for in defining controversial political phenomena they define their own roles as well.

It is often the most confidently held perceptions that are most confidently repudiated at later times or in other situations: beliefs in possession by demons, in the responsibility for initiating a war, in the definition of adherents to a political cause as subversive or irrational. Clearly, neither the confidence with which a political belief is held nor its contemporary popularity is an indicator of its validity, though it is an indicator of its reality. Indeed, the intensity with which a problematic definition of an issue engages some people usually signals the level of intensity with which a conflicting definition engages others. In such instances, both groups may well feel and act all the more single-mindedly because they must overcome their own awareness of the problematic nature of their position. The Freudian ego-defensive processes, especially repression and displacement, are one way of labeling the dynamics of contradictory cognitive structures. Conflicting cognitions are therefore a compelling device for marshaling political support or opposition and at the same time a psychological mechanism through which people can live with policies they resent or resist.

Consider how observations of "fact" rest, at least partly, upon ideological presuppositions when people with authority, privileges, status, or money justify the denial of these values to others. The view that public school students, prisoners, and hospitalized mental patients benefit from discipline, control, denial of autonomy and civil rights, and involuntary incarceration, or that generous welfare benefits encourage sloth and dependency, justifies the authority and roles of their keepers and the interest of citizens in minimizing tax levies. Yet it is surely too harsh a judgment that the hundreds of thousands of middle-class citizens, social workers, teachers and school administrators, mental health professionals, prison administrators, and guards who hold this view of the future outcomes of their actions are self-consciously or cynically advancing it as a ploy for retaining their authority, privileges, or income. Problematic beliefs about *future* outcomes become very real for those whose interests they justify, while perceptions of immediate outcomes that are incongruent with those beliefs remain dim. This is a recurring phenomenon in the relations of authorities with those they control. By the same token, once it is taken for granted that the politically powerless are victims of their social circumstances and potentially just as competent as their keepers, observations reinforce that conclusion, which becomes very real.[10] It is, regrettably, a frequent finding of policy research that good intentions are nullified by unintended consequences. One way of showing that cognitions are problematic is to examine such consequences.

Multiple Realities as Threats

Later chapters call attention to many widely held political beliefs that are problematic because research calls the belief into question

[10] Some social psychologists deal with the form of problematic perception that places the causes of disturbing behavior in the traits of individuals or groups

or because others hold conflicting beliefs just as firmly or because there is no definitive way of verifying or falsifying either view. The liberal who perceives public education in America as a liberating influence is offended and threatened by its definition as a form of indoctrination or stultification, though both views are common in popular talk and in academic research. There is evidence of a sort for both perceptions, permitting observation to reflect the presuppositions of the observer. Neitzsche rejected what he called the "dogma of immaculate perception."

Any study that focuses on the problematic character of strongly held beliefs is accordingly bound to offend many people because it calls attention to the warrant for conclusions different from those the believer accepts as rational and empirically based. It also calls attention to the warrant for a wider range of observations than those conventionally defined as adequate. To the intelligence tester, the social scientist who examines the problematic character of test results is not contributing to knowledge but threatening a scientific approach.

It is instructive to consider which kinds of observations of social problems readily come to attention and remain vivid and which kinds are seldom noticed; for the exercise is a reminder that beliefs about common issues that seem to be empirically based depend partly on values and the suppression of data.

The word "welfare" evokes an image of a drain upon the community's tax revenues and of chiselers who do not like to work. It just as effectively masks other "facts" that would lead many to a different view of proper policy toward the poor: the research evidence that the poor want to work, widespread malnutrition due to poverty, the terrors and loneliness of poverty, the discouragement of eligible people by welfare agencies and by cumbersome or humiliating procedures. Self-conscious examination of the highlighting and masking of observations about other social problems in the light of pertinent research similarly points to the selective character of observation and to the reflection of that selectivity, rather than its exposure, in public opinion and in some conventional social research.

Political facts are especially vivid and memorable when the terms

under the rubric of "attribution theory." See Harold Kelly, "Attribution: Perceiving the Causes of Behavior," *Nebraska Symposium on Motivation, 1967*, ed. David Levine (Lincoln: University of Nebraska Press, 1967), pp. 192–240.

that denote them depict a personified threat: an enemy, deviant, criminal, or wastrel. Facts are easily ignored when they deal with statistical probabilities involving people whose characteristics are not known. Such individuals are not threats and they have no features with which observers identify. The anonymous but certain victims of bomb test fallout, of problematic labeling as deviants, of bureaucratic errors, are not real in the vivid sense that the stereotype of a junkie or maniac is. Nor does the certainty that the first kind of problem will bring more harm than the second make it a "fact" psychologically. It carries grave social and economic consequences but minimal political consequences, while personified threats are politically potent regardless of the seriousness or triviality of their impact upon people's lives. The personified threat, no matter how atypical, marshals public support for controls over a much larger number of ambiguous cases symbolically condensed into the threatening stereotype.

Because the whole point of studies of political symbolism is to examine the evocation of alternative cognitions, they polarize readers who are committed to their own perceptions. The problem is not serious when research focuses upon the problematic character of the beliefs of people living in alien cultures or the beliefs of dissenters and rebels. Such analysis is consonant with the cognitions into which everyone is socialized and with the roles the great majority must play. An examination of dominant symbols encounters wider resistance. Indeed, some are likely to confuse a statement that an alternative to their own perception is tenable with a claim that that alternative is reality. If the analytic utility of the notion of multiple realities is growing, it is still far from common.

The Focus on Official Language

I concentrate on what is problematic in the language of public officials and of conventional professionals rather than in the language of their critics. If I want to analyze political symbols in the actual operations of regimes, rather than in the language of their critics, that focus is obviously necessary. That is an adequate rationale, though there is admittedly a sense in which it is also a rationalization, for I *am* critical of these institutions and find it congenial to examine the processes through which symbols evoke strong political beliefs even when there is little warrant for the self-assurance.

My own preferences among alternative patterns of belief about social problems are usually clear. To try to conceal them would only produce a *dramaturgy* of objectivity, a stance that has contaminated too many studies, discouraging the self-critical and tentative posture that investigators and critics need to maintain. A claim of value-free research would be especially inappropriate in a study whose purpose is to analyze the ties between observation and social situations and to probe the range of perceptions about social issues that people take to be fact.

Nor do I mean that any set of cognitions is as good as any other. When two major studies, employing different methods, conclude that welfare benefits do not detract from the incentive to work, for example, I have greater confidence in that conclusion than in the belief, very likely more widespread in America, that welfare discourages the poor from taking jobs. The significant point, nonetheless, is that there *are* contradictory beliefs and that their concurrence has identifiable nonobvious consequences for governmental action and for public support and opposition.

I explore those consequences without pretending to demonstrate the validity of either position both because "validity" according to some particular set of assumptions is not relevant to this analysis, and because it is impossible here to explore exhaustively the complications and controversies respecting the many issues I draw upon as examples. There are large literatures on welfare policy, psychotherapy, educational policy, and labeling theory, and in each case the literature exemplifies contradictions in premises and controversial conclusions. Differences respecting conceptual frameworks, implicit premises, and norms yield diverse conclusions about the pertinence of data and the meaning of findings.

With her usual perspicacity, Hannah Arendt made the critical observation: "In politics, more than anywhere else, we have no possibility of distinguishing between being and appearance. In the realm of human affairs, being and appearance are indeed one and the same." [11] My focus, then, is upon multiple realities, not upon the determination of which position is real or realistic. We all play lan-

[11] Hannah Arendt, *On Revolution* (New York: Viking, 1963), p. 94.

guage games. The deductive logical form and the devices for verification recommended in conventional methods texts constitute one such game and yield one form of reality. I often accept that form myself because it is useful for some forms of understanding and social action, not because I see it as a means of discovering reality. Preferences respecting this epistemological issue doubtless reflect different degrees of willingness to tolerate ambiguity regarding the nature of the political world. There is no question that the analysis of evocative language and of multiple realities creates some vertiginous perspectives. Like the language forms I explore, the language in which I write is evocative. Reader and writer seem to be wandering through a hall of mirrors or clambering around the perspectives of a cubist political scene. But so are the political spectator and the political actor, and in view of that "fact," how can we best *really* see them?

Rhetorical Evocations

It is through metaphor, metonymy, and syntax that linguistic references evoke mythic cognitive structures in people's minds. This is hardly surprising, for we naturally define ambiguous situations by focusing on one part of them or by comparing them with familiar things.

A reference in an authoritative public statement or in a Social Security law to "training programs" for the unemployed is a metonymic evocation of a larger structure of beliefs: that job training is efficacious in solving the unemployment problem, that workers are unemployed because they lack necessary skills, that jobs are available for those trained to take them. Because each component of this interrelated set of beliefs is dubious, job training has been largely ineffective as a strategy for decreasing unemployment. But people who are anxious to fight unemployment and eager to believe the problem can be solved without drastic social change are ready to accept this kind of reassuring cue. In the same way, those who feel threatened by extant social institutions are disposed to accept the cognitive structure implied by the term "political prisoner"; for the definition of a larcenist or drug addict as a political prisoner implies a great deal more: a polity that drives those it deprives to desperate measures, law enforcers who suppress dissidents, prisoners who are victims rather than criminals, and an observer who cherishes the role of radical.

Metaphor is equally effective and probably even more common in the linguistic evocation of political myths. The psychologist Theodore Sarbin has suggested that when Theresa of Avila referred in the seventeenth century to the problems of emotionally disturbed people as being like an illness, she used a metaphor that ultimately became a myth.[12] In view of anthropological evidence that cultures differ in what they define as mental abnormality and other studies demonstrating the social basis of such labeling, many social scientists believe, like Sarbin, that the judgment involved in calling someone "schizophrenic" is moral, not medical. Yet the metaphor of "mental illness" has become a myth widely accepted by laymen and conventional psychiatrists. It is used to deny freedom and dignity to people who already suffer from too little of either, and it is sometimes used to enforce conformity to Communist Party norms in the Soviet Union and to middle-class norms in the United States. At the same time it encourages treatment for some who are distressed or distraught. Sarbin suggests that movement from metaphor to myth is a common social phenomenon. It is especially common as a political phenomenon.

Even the syntax of a sentence can evoke a whole structure of beliefs, perhaps in more subtle and powerful fashion than metonymy and metaphor do. I have discussed the significance of form in political language in some detail elsewhere [13] and so refer to it here only in passing. When politicians and government officials appeal for public support for policies or candidates, the *form* of their statements conveys the message that public opinion is influential, and it does so both for those who accept the particular appeal and for those who do not, regardless of the content of the statement. If an appeal for support is made, then support obviously counts.

The form of legal language also conveys a reassuring message regardless of its content. Because the language of statutes, constitutions, and treaties consists of definitions and of specific commands to judges, administrative officials, and the general public to behave

[12] Theodore R. Sarbin, "Schizophrenia Is a Myth, Born of Metaphor, Meaningless," *Psychology Today* 6 (June 1972): 18 ff.; Theodore R. Sarbin, "On the Futility of the Proposition That Some People Be Labeled Mentally Ill," *Journal of Consulting Psychology* 31 (1967): 448, 451.

[13] Edelman, *The Symbolic Uses of Politics*, chap. 7.

in ways specified by elected representatives of the people, its very form offers reassurance of popular sovereignty and the rule of law. Lawyers take the ambiguity of legal language for granted in their practice, constantly disputing the meaning of terms; but to the general public legal language symbolizes precision and clarity in specifying the will of legislatures and constitutional conventions. Lawyers themselves typically see it in this reassuring way when they are making Fourth of July speeches or discussing government in the abstract rather than arguing in court that an adversary's interpretation of the law is mistaken. Here again is evidence of the pervasive ambivalence characteristic of our political beliefs and of the availability of alternative political myths to enable us to play alternative roles and to resolve difficult contradictions.

Given a strong incentive toward a pattern of belief, it is most effectively engendered by a term that implies the rest of the cognitive structure without explicitly calling attention to it. To declare that the cause of poverty is the laziness of its victims is to arouse questions and doubts and to call counterevidence to mind. Similarly, an explicit statement that welfare administrators and social workers are coping competently and effectively with the poverty problem or that economic institutions are not involved in it or responsible for it arouses skepticism, not belief. But a reference to the "welfare problem," to "the need for counseling welfare recipients," or to a "work test" as a condition for welfare unconsciously creates or reinforces a "pattern one" myth in those whose interests that belief serves. It justifies a role and self-conception they cherish.

As people hear the news every day, they fit it into the themes comprising the structural elements of each form of myth. Experiences are likely to reinforce the same meanings and illustrate them rather than change them.

Crime, mental illness, and other persistent social problems engender the same set of contradictory beliefs as poverty does: in terms of pathological institutions or in terms of pathological individuals. That is hardly surprising in view of their close link to poverty.

Rebellion engenders a belief in some that the rebels are a small minority, that they are subversive of the good society, or that they are dupes of radicals or aliens. At the same time, rebellion is perceived as the only viable form of politics for people denied influence through conventional means; as a heroic struggle for equality, liberty, justice, or survival; as growing spontaneously from manifest grievances; and usually as all of these. These are the culturally sanctioned explanations for forceful resistance to established authority, and each reflects fears and hopes everyone shares in some degree. They recur as rebellion does, regardless of the circumstances of particular uprisings. The incompatible definitions coexist as social lore, as the core of separate and shifting cognitive structures, and as rationalizations for governmental policies.

Nonviolent unconventionality produces its own set of recurring cognitive reactions. People who adopt unconventional manners, dress, speech, or social practices evoke fears of disorder, cultural breakdown, and anarchy and also bring appreciation of their individuality, spontaneity, and gift for self-expression. The alternative possibilities can rationalize any individual posture and any public policy.

The following generalizations about the structure of political beliefs seem warranted: (1) For any pattern of beliefs about a controversial issue, the various components of the cognitive structure (beliefs about the cause of the problem, the roles of authorities, the classification of people according to levels of merit, the effective remedies) reinforce one another and evoke one another. (2) Beliefs regarding social problems conventionally classified as different (crime, poverty, mental illness) include the same fundamental themes. (3) Conflicting cognitions remain available for use as groups or individuals need them to resolve tensions. (4) The actions governments take to cope with social problems often contradict, as well as reflect, the beliefs used to rationalize those actions. While claiming to rehabilitate prisoners and the emotionally disturbed, authorities also constrain and punish them. While claiming to help the poor, public welfare agencies also control them and take pains to limit the help they offer. Governmental rhetoric and action, taken together, comprise an elaborate dialectical structure, reflecting the beliefs, the tensions, and the ambivalences that flow from social inequality and conflicting interests.

Ambivalence is not compromise or indecisiveness. Banal language evocative of fears, hopes, or personal interests engenders firm, single-minded cognitions that change with altered social situations. That political spectators are rarely in a position to express anything but a dichotomous choice doubtless encourages this outcome. They cannot divide their vote in proportion to their ambivalence. They must choose either to accept or defy the draft, to support a demonstration or fail to do so.

The distinction between beliefs and perceptions that are self-consciously tentative and those that are dogmatic is fundamental. Dogmatic believers reject information incompatible with their cherished opinions, but people who are sensitive to the tentative nature of their opinions take pains to seek out conflicting evidence. Identifiable forms of political language systematically evoke one or the other posture.

More generally, the challenge is to discover how language and gestures are transformed into complex cognitive structures. I try to throw some light on that process by examining everyday reactions to social problems from a number of different perspectives: by analyzing the dialectical character of persistent explanations of social problems and recurring actions to cope with them; by studying recurring categorizations in the language in which laymen, authorities, administrators, and professionals discuss social problems; by examining the linguistic evocation of certainty and tentativeness, of loyalty to authority, of commitment to inquiry, and of resort to resistance; and by exploring the power of alternative categories to justify alternative allocations of values.

The Authority, Language, and Ideology of the Helping Professions

The helping professionals (in psychiatry, social work, teaching) are crucial influences upon beliefs and political actions regarding poverty and related problems, for they present themselves, and are widely accepted, as legitimate authorities on the causes of these problems and on how to treat their victims. Their professional language and treatments shape public beliefs about which forms of behavior are acceptable. These professions authoritatively define the deserving, the undeserving, the competent, and the pathological; and in doing so they define themselves. Most of the poor, like most of the nonpoor, accept their definitions of people and situations, at least ambivalently.

The helping professions exemplify the tie between language and cognition in a way that is readily accessible to observation and analysis. Their categorizations become the standard rationale for governmental policies affecting the poor as individuals and as a social "problem." Professional labels of deviance also reflect and reinforce public anxiety, encouraging the problematic categorization of large numbers of people whose labels fit stereotypes but whose behavior may not. A woman whose poverty makes her angry or despondent becomes a different political symbol after a psychiatrist defines her as a "hysteric"; she now symbolizes individual sickness, not a malfunctioning economy.

Because the categorizations are based upon unacknowledged ideological premises, there are schisms within the professions, with dissenting professionals and conventional ones criticizing alleged biases in each other's language. The professional literature is therefore a ready source of examples of the alternative cognitive possibilities inherent in language and actions affecting the poor.

A radical sees as obvious bias (or as self-serving rationalization) the conventional psychiatrist's view that "disturbed behavior" stems from individual defects rather than from defects in economic and social institutions, just as the psychiatrist sees the radical view as bias or as rationalization. Each view reflects the definition of people and situations with which it starts, and each brings consequences that are reflected in personal ambivalence, in cognitive contradictions, and in public policies.

Social scientists, and a large segment of the public, have grown sensitive and allergic to agitational political rhetoric and to the ambiguities of such terms as "democracy" and "communist." The *fundamental* influences upon political beliefs flow, however, from language that is not perceived as political at all but nonetheless structures perceptions of status, authority, merit, deviance, and the causes of social problems. Here is a level of politics that conventional political science rarely touches, but one that explains a great deal of the overt political maneuvering and governmental action that focuses public attention.

Categorization, Perception, and Politics

Perception involves categorization.[1] To place an object in one class of things rather than another establishes its central characteristics and creates assumptions about matters that are not seen. To see a person as a "welfare official" highlights some of his or her activities, assumes others, and masks still others that are not part of the welfare official role, even though he or she may perform them. Linguistic categorization evokes a large part of everyone's political world because neither the public nor news reporters can observe most actions of public officials and because categorizations give meaning both to what is observed and to what is assumed.

Another characteristic of the political spectator reinforces the same effect. By definition, he or she is not an actor whose policies have tangible consequences. It is not feedback about what political actions achieve that matters to the spectator of the political scene, but the

Parts of this chapter are revisions of Murray Edelman, "Language and Social Problems," *Society* 12 (July–August 1975): 14–21. © 1975 Transaction, Inc.
[1] Cf. Noam Chomsky, *Cartesian Linguistics* (New York: Harper and Row, 1966), pp. 123–31.

efficacy of his or her beliefs in stilling anxieties or raising hopes. Verbal categorization rather than physical action defines his involvement.

Recent work in phenomenology brings an enhanced appreciation of the power of language, especially in ambiguous situations. Maurice Merleau-Ponty points out that just as the gestures of an actor playing Lear present Lear, not the actor, to his audience, so a term *is* the thought it evokes, not a tool for expressing a preexisting thought. In the act of speaking or writing, people create ideas in themselves of which they were not aware before they were expressed; and in responding to others' language, auditors and readers similarly engender cognitions in themselves, thereby communicating.

> Thought and expression . . . are simultaneously constituted . . . . The spoken word is a genuine gesture, and it contains its meaning in the same way as the gesture contains its. This is what makes communication possible.[2]

The crucial function of language in abstract thought and in conceiving situations other than objects immediately in view is also evident from the behavior of sufferers from aphasia. Aphasia is loss of the ability to express ideas, resulting from brain damage. Aphasic patients cannot make statements about possible situations that do not actually exist, nor group objects according to color or other common properties when asked to do so. It is only in naming situations or characteristics that they are conceived, communicated, and perceived; and it is because naming also amounts to categorizing and abstracting (which it does not for aphasics) that actors and spectators on the political scene create aspects of that scene that are not observable and may be nonexistent.

Consider an example that clarifies how fundamentally categorizations shape both what we see and what we do not see in the political world. In every state mental hospital there are people, classified as "paranoid schizophrenics," who think they could save the world if they were only heeded. Those who know their categorization as paranoid schizophrenics naturally perceive something ir-

---

[2] Maurice Merleau-Ponty, *Phenomenology of Perception* (London: Routeledge and Kegan Paul, 1962), p. 183.

rational in those patients. But a rather large proportion of the population, especially a great number who hold, or aspire to, high political office, and a great number who are attached to a political ideology, also think they could save the world if they were only heeded. And, judging from the fruits of their efforts over many centuries of recorded history, they are no more likely to be either right or wrong than the "schizophrenics." Much of the population perceives them as incompetent if a psychiatrist classifies them as sick, but as more competent than the average citizen if they hold high public office. The *Pentagon Papers* show that the intelligent, highly educated, experienced policymakers of the Kennedy and Johnson administrations were convinced that military intervention in Vietnam would stop the spread of "world communism" through a war that would be won quickly at small cost, and that they continued to believe it after several years of counterevidence—exemplifying a degree of reconstruction of reality few "psychotics" can ever have matched. The example could be multiplied thousands of times from a survey of political history.

Political and ideological debate consists very largely of efforts to win acceptance of a particular categorization of an issue in the face of competing efforts in behalf of a different one; but because participants are likely to see it as a dispute either about facts or about individual values, the linguistic (that is, social) basis of perceptions is usually unrecognized. The authoritative status of the source of a categorization makes his or her definition of the issue more readily acceptable for an ambivalent public called upon to react to an ambiguous situation.

So far as political beliefs are concerned, the most potent categorizations almost certainly are visions of the future. The typification of a new leader of a powerful rival country as sympathetic and peace-loving evokes a future marked by detente and cooperation in the two countries' dealings with each other. The depiction of the poor as incompetent or as breeding faster than the middle class, perhaps through a metaphoric reference to rule by mobs, creates a future in which the unworthy dominate the virtuous. Such cognitions coexist with contradictory beliefs and perceptions. The person who expresses fears of the high birth rates of the poor may intermittently perceive them as infusing welcome variety into the national culture or providing needed manpower for industry and the army.

For the politician these problematic and ambiguous categorizations offer a challenge and an opportunity. For mass publics they are a recurring stimulus to anxiety or to hope.

Only rarely, however, are such evocations original. They are ordinarily an instance of what Alfred Schutz calls "a treasure house of readymade pre-constituted types and characteristics, all socially derived and carrying along an open horizon of explored content." [3] As typifications, they focus upon what is alike among situations, issues, events, or persons, but they ignore whatever is unique. Most thinking has to be of this sort, for attention to the special characteristics of every situation would obviously require more time, energy, and skill than any human being can command. The consequence of perceiving typifications that are evoked unconsciously is that political beliefs normally reinforce one or another preestablished social consensus. They are unlikely to take account of the unique and critical features of an issue, though it is exactly those features that render the issue susceptible to effective resolution. Shared typifications nonetheless justify shared causes.

The Linguistic Structuring of Social Problems

Consider the political implications of our conventional mode of naming and classifying the most common social "problems": poverty, crime, mental illness, occupational illness, drug abuse, and inadequate education. We establish separate departments of government to deal with these supposedly distinct problems (departments of welfare, criminal justice, education, health, for example), and staff them with people trained to focus upon a particular set of symptoms and to believe in a distinctive set of causes for each of them. Such a classification evokes beliefs and perceptions that we normally accept uncritically, precisely because they are generated subtly by the terms used to designate them. The classification scheme implies, first, that these various problems are distinct from one another, with different causes, just as they have separate symptoms.

A considerable body of research suggests that this premise is

[3] Alfred Schutz, "Common-Sense and Scientific Interpretation of Human Action," *Philosophy and Phenomenological Research* 14 (September 1953): 10.

simplistic and distorting because all of these problems can be seen as flowing largely from the functioning of economic institutions. If economic institutions functioned without unemployment, poorly paid work, degrading work, or inadequate industrial pension and health programs, there would manifestly be very little poverty. Is poverty, then, a problem of "welfare" policy or of economic institutions? Contradictory cognitions are available for use; those who accept the research pointing to the second view conclude that to blame the problems of the poor on welfare policy is to confuse the symptom with the cause.

A recent study of *Work in America* finds that the work adults do is usually central in their lives, critical to their self-conceptions and their self-esteem; but this research also shows that many workers at all occupational levels find their work so stultifying and demeaning that it is a major contributor to physical illness, emotional disturbance, alcoholism, and drug abuse.[4] This and many other studies suggest that the various social "problems" we treat separately are very largely symptoms of the same problem: an economic system that produces too few jobs, too little income and security, and too few opportunities for self-fulfillment.

Terms like "mental illness," "criminal," and "drug abuse" focus attention on the alleged weakness and pathology of the individual, while diverting attention from their pathological social and economic environments—a belief about causation that is partially accurate at best and therefore a dubious premise on which to base public policies. In consequence we maintain prisons that contribute to crime as a way of life for many of their inmates, mental hospitals that contribute to "mental illness," as a way of life for *their* inmates, and high rates of recidivism for all these "problems." But the names by which we refer to people and their problems continue, subtly but potently, to keep the attention of authorities, professionals, and the general public focused upon hopes for rehabilitation of the individual and to divert attention from those results of established policies that are counterproductive.

Conventional names for social problems evoke other dubious beliefs and perceptions. The "welfare" label connotes to many that the problem lies in a public dole, which encourages laziness. This

---

[4] U.S. Department of Health, Education and Welfare, *Work in America* (Washington, D.C.: U.S. Government Printing Office, 1972).

widespread belief about the cause of poverty is further reinforced by other political terms, such as the "work test" provisions widely publicized in the 1967 and 1971 Social Security Act amendments. Our language creates a picture of hundreds of thousands of welfare recipients refusing a plentiful supply of productive work, when pertinent research shows (1) that only a very small percentage of the recipients are physically able to work, and even these typically cannot find jobs, with unemployment levels running between 5 and 8 percent of the labor force at best and much higher in the localities where the recipients are concentrated; and (2) that welfare benefits do not detract from work incentive.[5]

Because public policies and rhetoric can create misleading beliefs about the causes and the nature of these problems, they also ensure that the problems will not be dealt with as effectively as they might be. While the expenditures, the layers of bureaucracy, and the numbers of professionals dealing with crime, welfare, emotional disturbance, and illness increase, the number of people who suffer from them also continues to increase.[6] Rehabilitation and rational solution of problems occurs very largely in rhetoric. Such everyday language and the myths it evokes permit us to live with ourselves and with our problems; they also guarantee that perceptions of threats and of efforts to overcome them will maintain social tension, anxiety, and continued susceptibility to verbal cues that help legitimize government policies regardless of their effectiveness.

Prevailing categorizations of these problems create cognitive structures even more intricate than this discussion has so far suggested. They imply that the inadequacies of the poor and the waywardness of the delinquent are changeable and that governmental and professional rewards, punishments, and treatments will change them; but the classification scheme by the same token defines economic institutions as a fixed part of the scene, not an issue to be confronted. In this way, the name for a problem also creates beliefs about what conditions public policy can change and what it cannot touch.

Still another facet of this cognitive structure deals with the statuses

---

[5] Leonard Goodwin, *Do the Poor Want to Work?* (Washington, D.C.: The Brookings Institution, 1972); U.S. Department of Health, Education, and Welfare, *Report of the New Jersey Graduated Work Incentive Experiment* (Washington, D.C.: U.S. Government Printing Office, 1973).

[6] For a trenchant discussion and documentation of this point, see Robert Alford, *Health Care Politics* (Chicago: University of Chicago Press, 1975).

of people. When we name and classify a problem, we unconsciously establish the status and the roles of those involved with it, including their self-conceptions. If the problem is an economic system that yields inadequate monetary and psychological benefits, then the working poor and the unemployed are victims; but if the problem is personal pathology, they are lazy or incompetent. The economic elite may be lucky or unscrupulous or they may be resourceful and industrious. Those who refuse to play conventional roles may be independent or moral or self-protective or they may be mentally ill or immoral; and so on. How the problem is named involves alternative scenarios, each with its own facts, value judgments, and emotions. The self-conceptions that are a part of these contradictory cognitive structures explain the tenacity and passion with which people who are intimately involved cling to them and interpret developments so as to make them consonant with a particular structure; for the choice of a configuration of beliefs has profound consequences for the individual: his role and status, his power and responsibilities, his ideology, and what counts as success for her or him.

No structure of political cognitions can persist unless others share it, reinforcing the common belief. No person is a success or a problem, no issue distinctive or important, unless others see them that way. The authority and status of public officials, politicians, and helping professionals therefore depend on public acceptance of their norms regarding merit and deviance and of their definitions of issues. The authority's insecurity and need for public support is correlative with the public's anxiety about the problems authorities present themselves as able to handle.

The Evocation of Mythical Populations as Reference Groups

Perhaps the archetypical device for influencing political opinion is the evocation of beliefs about the problems, the intentions, or the moral condition of people whose very existence is problematic, but who become the benchmarks by which real people shape their political beliefs and perceptions.

Sometimes such formulations are essentially accurate. When, in the trough of the Great Depression, Franklin Roosevelt referred to "one-third of a nation ill-nourished, ill-clad, and ill-housed," he was manifestly employing rhetoric to marshal support for policies he favored; but his assertion about a sizable fraction of the American people was not an exaggeration by observations widely made and little challenged.

Politicians' statements about unobservable people are often either impossible to verify or quite clearly invalid. When, in the midst of widespread public objection to the Vietnam War, Richard Nixon referred to a "silent majority" that supported his hawkish war policy, his allegation was dubious in light of pertinent research.[7] Its function was to evoke a reference group other than the plainly visible and nonsilent one for the large numbers of people who were torn or uncertain regarding their position on the war. For such a purpose a "majority" that cannot be observed because it is "silent" is ideal. For anyone looking for a reason to support the President and the war, the "silent majority" serves its purpose even if it does not exist.

Anxious people reliant on dubious and conflicting cues can choose from available public messages the one that supports a policy consistent with their economic interests or ideological bent. Groups trying to marshal support for a position therefore benefit from making public statements that will justify the positions of their potential supporters. The facts regarding controversial political issues are typically so complex and so ambiguous that it is easy to find a set of allegations that both serve this rationalizing function and are not manifestly untrue. They can be deliberate lies and sometimes are; they are often interpretations their audience would recognize as dubious if it knew enough about the observations on which they are based; and sometimes they are accurate. As influences on political opinion, however, their verifiability is less important than their availability, in view of the setting of anxiety for many and ambiguity for all in which controversial policy formation takes place.

Statistics evoke mythical reference groups too, often in a nonobvious way. Why is it so helpful to an incumbent administration that the month's unemployment statistics show a downturn and so useful to the political opposition when they show an upturn? People suffer if they are unemployed no matter what general trends the government statistics show, and their personal experiences are cer-

[7] John E. Mueller, "Trends in Popular Support for the Wars in Korea and Vietnam," *American Political Science Review* 65 (June 1971): 358–75.

tainly more critical to their beliefs, feelings, and political behavior than news accounts of economic trends. The point is that the statistics do provide the key benchmark for the overwhelming majority who are *not* directly affected by unemployment. Anxiety about their own job security and that of their friends and relatives is widespread; so cues about an incumbent administration's performance strike close to home. In this case, too, the validity of the cue is problematic, for the official statistics regularly understate the unemployment level by ignoring underemployment and by failing to count as unemployed people so discouraged with job hunting that they do not actively seek work; and official rhetoric always overstates the role of government when conditions improve. The statistics serve a need regardless of whether they are misleading, and they do it all the better because they are presented as "hard data." They evoke a belief that the unemployed population is rising or declining in size, that a particular monthly increase is an aberration or that it is part of a long-term trend. They therefore engender public support or distrust among people who are anxious about the state of the economy and about their own futures.

In the same way many other kinds of time series statistics evoke fictional reference groups and benchmarks. A decline in the rate of increase in reported crimes reassures anxious people that the government is reestablishing law and order; but such a statistical decline is usually an artifact of the method of computing it (the same increase in crime every year obviously yields a marked decline in the rate) or of the zeal of law enforcement agencies in reporting crimes.

Statistics are so effective in shaping political support and opposition that governments sometimes publicize statistics that have little or no bearing on an issue creating anxiety, either because none that do have a bearing are available or because the pertinent ones point in the wrong direction. If a Southeast Asian war turns out to be a disaster, a modicum of public support can still be maintained by disseminating enemy "body counts" suggesting that ten times as many enemy as American soldiers are being killed every week or month. As visible and easily understood "hard data," the statistics mask both their lack of pertinence to the question of who is "winning" the war and the fabrication of the figures by field commanders whose promotions depend upon the reporting of high enemy body counts. This example is an extreme one, but for that reason it illustrates all the better the possibility of creating persuasive benchmarks for anxious people eager to find a reason to believe whatever will serve their interests or their ideological inclinations.

Inconspicuous or implicit references can create the impression public policies are helping the needy even when they chiefly benefit the affluent. For at least four decades American legislation purporting to help "the family farmer" has transferred millions of dollars from the taxpayers to corporate farming enterprises while helping to drive the family farmer into the city. A combination of sympathy for the small farmer and of eagerness to entrust policymaking to those who know how to deal with problems endows a casual term with the power to engender cognitions that are politically potent whether or not they are valid.

Sometimes the ideological appeal of a symbol is apparently stronger than the observable conditions in which people live their everyday lives. One study notices, for example, that welfare recipients almost always refer to welfare receipients as "they" rather than "we"; and that a majority of people receiving welfare benefits favor midnight searches of the homes of recipients and compulsory budget counseling.[8] These people may well ignore their own experiences and focus upon a mythical population of welfare parasites created by the language of their political adversaries.

Such symbolic devices are not omnipotent. People often resist them when they run counter to self-evident or perceived interests; and many manifestly do not.

The Categorization of Enemies

One of the most frequent recurring forms of political categorization is the definition of some large group of people as so serious a threat that their physical existence, their most characteristic ways of thought and feeling, or both must be exterminated or ruthlessly repressed. The genocidal killing of thousands (in the Nazi case, millions) of people, the torture of political prisoners, witchhunts against subversives or people thought to be in league with the devil, and the

---

[8] Frances F. Piven and Richard A. Cloward, *Regulating the Poor* (New York: Vintage, 1971), p. 172.

beating of political protesters while arresting them virtually everywhere are some of the more conspicuous examples of a form of cognition that has always victimized a large part of the world's population with the enthusiastic or tacit support of many others. In his study of the Kent State shootings James Michener reported that "the mother of two Ohio college students advocated firing on students even for minor practices, such as going barefoot and wearing long hair." [9]

The most intense animus has always been directed against people later recognized as innocent of the evil contemporaries saw in them: the Jews in Nazi Germany and in Russia at the turn of the century, the heretics under the Inquisition, the Catholics during the Know-Nothing persecutions of the 1830s, the American Indians in the nineteenth century, the counterculture in the 1960s. Adversaries who hurt, as distinct from those who serve a psychological and political function for their antagonists, arouse a different form of response, and even though the definition of the innocent as enemies recurs, each instance is later regarded as an unfortunate exception; for it is hard to accept that common beliefs rationalize punitiveness.

Other manifestations of the same psychological phenomenon may not at first seem quite of the same order, but only because they are even more common. There is often a high degree of punitiveness toward such victimless "crimes" as unconventional sex practices, the use of drugs, and attempted suicide. Fear of the poor and alien is manifestly close to the surface for many, and it grows especially intense when the poor or alien behave unconventionally. There is ready support for restrictions upon their autonomy that authorities define as "help," even when they entail incarceration.

Low status in itself seems to encourage the perception of threat to society. Theodore Sarbin observes that the word "dangerous" "seems to have been shaped out of linguistic roots that signified *relative position* in a social structure."

> Those persons or groups that threaten the existing power structure are dangerous. In any historical period, to identify an individual whose status is that of a member of the "dangerous classes," . . . the label "criminal" has been handy. . . . The construct, criminal, is not used to

---

[9] Reported in American Friends Service Committee, *Struggle for Justice* (New York: Hill and Wang, 1971), p. 155.

classify the performers of all legally defined delicts, only those whose position in the social structure qualifies them for membership in the dangerous classes.[10]

If the ideas of criminality and poverty are associated linguistically, they are even more obviously associated in the definition and punishment of crime, supporting Sarbin's point. While white-collar crime (price fixing, embezzlement, illegal trade practices) is widely regarded as an understandable extension of normal business practice, hardly dangerous, and rarely penalized severely, the crimes of the poor (larceny, assault) become evidence of inherent dangerousness and are far more severely punished, though they hurt only a small fraction of the number of people injured by white-collar crime and rarely hurt their victims as severely or with as lasting effects.

There are some striking characteristics of the "enemies" who engender intense emotion and punitiveness. First, a large part of the population does not see them as enemies at all. The very fact that their categorization is controversial seems to intensify the fears of those who do perceive them as threats, for their own rationality is at stake. Belief in the reality of this enemy becomes the test of their credibility and the touchstone of their self-esteem. Second, the group defined as the enemy is a relatively powerless segment of the population and often a small minority. Third, the enemies are thought to operate through covert activities. They may look like students, businessmen, or ordinary political dissenters, but they are really engaged in secret subversion, dangerous to others and themselves. To categorize them as doing evil covertly is to ignore their visible human qualities and so to rationalize their eradication.

This mode of definition is better understood when it is contrasted with the political definition and perception of ordinary adversaries. An opposition engaging in visible hostile tactics calls for tactical and strategic countermoves, not repression. The opponent's talent for planning and susceptibility to error are taken into account, each side trying to see the situation from the other's perspective in order to better anticipate his or her strategy. The perception of the opponent as an ordinary human being, with a human being's propensity for calculation and for error, accounts for attitudes and actions in such

[10] Theodore R. Sarbin, *The Myth of the Criminal Type* (Middletown, Conn.: Wesleyan University, Center for Advanced Studies, 1969). Quoted in American Friends Service Committee, *Struggle for Justice*, pp. 77–78.

confrontations. But the evocation of an alien who does evil covertly defines him as inhuman and uncanny (to borrow Freud's word for a similar form of perception). It is accordingly impossible to put oneself in his place and therefore impossible to see things from his perspective, bargain with him, or play games of strategy with him. Only repression can bring salvation.

I have examined these contrasting postures in terms of their psychological characteristics: perception, strategic calculation, expectation, role-taking, and feeling. The postures can also be understood as expressions of linguistic categorizations.[11] In the one case the opponent is classified as a human antagonist, endowed with intellectual equipment and limitations like our own, making it possible to "play games" with him, though the games may be serious and even lethal. Bosses, opponents in sports, labor unions, rival political interest groups and political parties, adversaries in legal actions, and enemies in war are usually categorized in this way. These are all visible people, engaged in the tactics that their labels as "sport competitors," "unions," "the British enemy," and so on connote. Enemies of the other sort bear labels that highlight the covert, inhuman, incalculabel qualities that make it impossible to deal with them as fellow human beings: "communist conspirator," nihilist, hard-core criminal, psychopath; or, in other ages and places, "witch," and "pactor with the devil." Metaphor and metonymy reinforce such perceptions by providing the anxious person with grounds for believing that all other right-minded people see and feel as he or she does.

Notice that it is *only* through names and other verbal signs that such nonvisible enemies are known and perceived. By definition they either act invisibly or their psychic malfunctions are internal. Linguistic reference engenders a "reality" that is not *phenomenologically* different from any other reality.

The Linguistic Generation of Assumptions

Some linguistic forms generate important beliefs that are uncritically and unconsciously taken for granted. In politics they frequently deal with such matters as the utility of a governmental pro-

---

[11] For a discussion of the view that the same phenomena are describable in terms of psychological traits or in terms of linguistic characteristics, see David Pears, *Ludwig Wittgenstein* (New York: Viking, 1970), pp. 149–78.

gram, who is responsible for its success or failure, or the salience of a course of action.

Consider some common examples. Campaigns urging car owners to drive safely, whether sponsored by a government agency or a trade association, focus attention on the driver as the cause of accidents: on his negligent or risky habits and his failure to keep his car in good working order. These campaigns divert public attention from information suggesting that automobile accidents are inevitable regardless of driver habits because the biological and psychological capacities of human beings are simply not adequate to cope with every unexpected circumstance that occurs on the road. Faulty design and engineering make them "unsafe at any speed"; but, beyond that, high horsepower, high speed limits, and hills and corners create situations with which the human brain and nervous system cannot be counted on to cope every time, no matter how careful the driver or how sound the car's mechanism. Whether or not a "drive safely" campaign makes drivers more careful, it creates an assumption about what the problem is and who is responsible for it that can be only partially valid. The focus upon the sinning driver takes for granted a great deal that needs skeptical analysis; and it does so with little controversy or inner doubt, for who can question the virtue of safe driving? This form of cognition is helpful to car manufacturers and to the highway lobby, while encouraging public criticism of the driver involved in an accident and creating self-doubt and guilt in drivers.

Vivid metaphors, sometimes including statistics respecting actual or hypothetical events, can create benchmarks that shape popular judgments of the success or failure of specific programs. An announcement that the government plans to reduce unemployment to the 6.8 percent level within a year or to hold an expected increase below the 7.5 percent level creates a benchmark of success against which future trends are then evaluated. Attention focuses on meeting the publicized goal, rather than upon the seven or eight million people who are still without jobs. Such a cognition even more completely takes for granted the institutional arrangements that make it probable that there will always be four to six million people unable to find work and others who have given up hope. Similar problematic benchmarks govern assumptions about whether a welfare or defense budget is reasonable or unreasonable and whether an authority's record of achievement is good or poor.

These examples involve incremental change in policy. A focus upon marginal change masks whatever underlies the increments and therefore what is most significant about a political situation. To publicize incremental changes in policy or in well-being is to establish categories that conceal the institutional context in which the problem is grounded. This form of structuring of a problem always produces symbolic or token gestures; for both officials and the public who are attentive to the increments perceive these as the core of the issue while remaining largely oblivious to whatever problems underlie the increments. Each symbolic gesture further reinforces the categorization scheme and the associated definition of the situation.

The Linguistic Reconstruction of Facts

Political facts that disturb people and produce conflict are often reconstructed so that they conform to general beliefs about what *should* be happening. Harold Garfinkel has given us an admirable analysis of the employment of this linguistic device by juries, showing that jurors reach agreement, when they do, by choosing to define what is fact, what is bias, and what is relevant to the issue in such a way as to make their decision conform to current social norms. The accepted norm, that is to say, defines the facts and their interpretation. As Garfinkel puts it, jurors decide

> between what is put on and what is truth . . . what is calculated and said by design; what is an issue and what was decided; between what is *still* an issue compared with what is irrelevant and will not be brought up again except by a person who has an axe to grind; between what is mere personal opinion and what any right-thinking person would have to agree to. . . . The decisions as to what "actually happened" provide jurors the grounds that they use in inferring the social support that they feel they are entitled to receive for the verdict they choose.[12]

[12] Harold Garfinkel, *Studies in Ethnomethodology* (Englewood Cliffs, N.J.: Prentice-Hall, 1967), pp. 106–7. Another study that offers revealing illustrations of the linguistic evocation of assumptions and reconstruction of facts, in this case in Nazi Germany and in East Germany, is Claus Mueller, *The Politics of Communication* (New York: Oxford University Press, 1973), pp. 24–42.

Analysis of any instance of the resolution of political conflict through agreement upon a verbal formula justifying an action reveals the same process of reconstruction of facts through ambiguity, highlighting of some aspects of the situation and concealment of others, substitution of a part of it for the whole, and the subtle evocation of what people want to see. Ever since it was established, the Federal Communications Commission (FCC) has given paramount weight in choosing among competing license applicants to the financial resources available to the applicant, so that wealthy individuals and successful corporations easily make a persuasive case, while people of moderate means, including minorities, dissenters, and radicals, are easily rejected. The Commission's justification is that radio listeners and television viewers will be hurt if the licensee uses poor equipment or goes bankrupt; the weighing of comparative financial resources therefore promotes "the public interest, convenience, or necessity," as required by the Communications Act of 1934.[13] Paramount weight to a more equal representation on the air of political perspectives could obviously be justified on the same ground. The FCC chooses among alternative definitions of what the key issues are, what is mere opinion, what any right-thinking person would have to agree to, and what will actually happen, just as jurors do. The majority of FCC appointees come from business backgrounds in which paramount concern with financing is taken for granted as right-thinking. Their official position, the reconstruction of their reasoning in terms of the ambiguous statutory formula, and the remoteness of the detailed issues from public attention allay doubts in public opinion and in the commissioners' minds.

It is not that jurors, commissioners, or the interested public simply forget or deny the issues that are obscured in the reconstruction. The reconstruction helps concerned people to accept problematic facts and interpretations of them and so to live with the decision. The ambiguity of the reconstructed set of issues enables each interested group to read into it whatever interpretation suits its purposes, while at the same time proclaiming to the less interested the welcome news that the issue has been resolved rationally.

Such implicit contradictions in official rhetoric justify governmental actions that would be resisted if their consequences were

[13] See Murray Edelman, *The Licensing of Radio Services in the United States, 1927 to 1947* (Urbana: University of Illinois Press, 1950).

explicitly stated. Vagrancy laws, for example, were initially enacted at a time when the breakdown of serfdom had depleted the supply of cheap labor available to landowners.[14] Even then it was apparently easier for people to live with the view that vagrants were potential troublemakers who needed control than with an explicit recognition that the criminal justice system was providing employers a docile and cheap labor supply. Such laws and their application by county sheriffs still help control dissenters and force them to take work that is offered, accomplishing a "publicly unmentionable goal"[15] by focusing upon a popular one: control of crime. As is usually true in such instances, the official justification has an ambiguous basis in fact. People without means of support may well violate the law if they are worried or desperate. The unstated issues are whether the many who have *not* violated the law should therefore be penalized and whether the appropriate remedy for those who have is prison or forced labor on terms free workers will not accept. The definition of the issue justifies these consequences, not by denying them, but by labeling poor people as criminals and so helping the general public, employers, and law enforcement officers to live with their qualms.

Dominant categories of speech and of thought define the economically successful and the politically powerful as meritorious, and the unsuccessful and politically deviant as mentally or morally inadequate. For the same reason, policies that serve the interests of the influential come to be categorized as routine and equitable outcomes of duly established governmental processes. Metaphor and syntax mask the amenability of these processes to unconscious (or conscious) manipulation in line with private advantage.

In winning public acceptance of policies, stress upon established governmental routines is critical, for these routines ("due process of law") are highly flexible in the motivations and outcomes they allow, but highly confining in the perceptions they engender. Motivations and outcomes may be self-serving, but their origin in elections, legislation, and judicial proceedings transmutes them into the public will. Even when authorities make anxious concessions to protesters who deliberately violate legal processes, they publicly define their actions as routine responses. In granting concessions to ghetto rioters

---

[14] American Friends Service Committee, *Struggle for Justice*, p. 40.
[15] The phrase is from Garfinkel, *Studies in Ethnomethodology*.

officials always deny that they are yielding to violence, and the vehemence of the denials is in proportion to their ambivalent recognition that that is what they are doing.

Perhaps the most common form of reconstruction of facts through language occurs through the ready assimilation into a clear or ideal typification of cases that are doubtful or different. Well-authenticated, widely publicized instances of fraud by welfare recipients make it easy to see the doubtful as clear. One study of beliefs about welfare recipients found that

> respondents in the study cited persons on relief more frequently than they mentioned any other category of people when they were asked to name persons who got more than they deserved. Approximately one third of the respondents in each class spontaneously mentioned mothers on relief, men on welfare, etc., as getting more than they deserved. And respondents from the lower-middle and laboring classes were more likely to complain of people on welfare than about the obviously wealthy people getting more than they deserve.[16]

Clearly, categorization does not simply create perceptions or misperceptions of others who are physically remote; it also influences dubious perceptions of others who are close by. The name for a category shapes beliefs and public policy, reconstructing the unique qualities of individual people, of social problems, and of policies into influential stereotypes.

The Linguistic Segmentation of the Political World

The various issues with which governments deal are highly interrelated in the contemporary world, though we are cued to perceive them as distinct. Because each day's news and each day's governmental announcements evoke anxieties and reassurances about specific "problems" perceived as separate from each other (foreign affairs, strikes, fuel shortages, food shortages, prices, party politics, and so on), our political worlds are segmented, disjointed, focused at any moment upon some small set of anxieties, even though each

[16] Melvin J. Lerner, "All the World Loathes a Loser," *Psychology Today* 5 (June 1971): 66.

such "issue" is a part of an increasingly integrated whole. Wars bring commodity shortages and rising prices, which in turn foment worker discontent and a search for enemies. Economic prosperity brings a decline in theft and vagrancy and an increase in white-collar crime, higher demands for fuel, and other ramifications. But our mode of referring to problems and policies creates for each of us a succession of crises, of respites, of separate grounds for anxiety and for hope. Where people do perceive links among issues, that perception itself is likely to be arbitrary and politically cued, for reasons already discussed. To experience the political world as a sequence of distinct events, randomly threatening or reassuring, renders people readily susceptible to cues, both deliberate and unintended; for the environment becomes unpredictable and people remain continuously anxious. In place of the ability to deal with issues in terms of their logical and empirical ties to one another, the language of politics encourages us to see them and to feel them as separate. This, too, is a formula for coping with them ineffectively, and that is bound to reinforce anxiety in its turn.

Created Worlds

It should be clear, then, that beliefs and perceptions based on problematic categorization are not the exceptions. In every significant respect political issues and actors assume characteristics that are symbolically cued. From subtle linguistic evocations and associated governmental actions we get a great many of our beliefs about what our problems are, their causes, their seriousness, our success or failure in coping with them, which aspects are fixed and which are changeable, and what impacts they have upon which groups of people. We are similarly cued into beliefs about which authorities can deal with which problems, the levels of merit and competence of various groups of the population, the benchmarks for judging public policies, and who are allies and who enemies. Though symbolic cues are not omnipotent, they go far toward defining the geography and the topography of everyone's political world.

National Crises and "Public Opinion" as Political Symbols

Two forms of problematic political categorization are critical in shaping beliefs: the definition of particular opinions as "public opinion" and the labeling of a set of events as a "crisis." Both these terms seem to be based on objective criteria and they appeal, respectively, to the most cherished common political hope (that the will of the people will prevail) and to the most feared common threat (that the polity is endangered by developments outside its control); hence, their evocative potency.

The Political Uses of National Crises

The word "crisis" connotes a development that is unique and threatening. When applied to a set of political events, the term is a form of problematic categorization because the development it highlights can also be perceived as recurring rather than singular and as an instance of arbitrary labeling. What events mean for policy formation depends on whether they are defined as exceptional or, alternatively, as one more set of incidents in a world that is chronically in crisis.

National crises, therefore, have their uses in shaping opinion, just as routine politics and chronic problems do. The twentieth century has seen economic, military, and social crises succeed one another and overlap with one another, and the foreseeable future will not be different. A worldwide food crisis is imminent, as are mineral shortages.

The controversies of each emergency mask the impact on our lives of continual crises. How does it influence politics that people are cued to see each crisis as unexpected and distinct?

The language in which each crisis is discussed is selective in what it highlights and in what it masks. To call a set of events a "crisis" implies certain beliefs that are also stressed in everyday political discussion:

1. This event is different from the political and social issues we routinely confront, different from other crises, and it occurs rarely.
2. It came about for reasons outside the control of political and industrial leaders, who are coping with it as best they can.
3. The crisis requires sacrifices in order to surmount it.

In the course of any crisis, these propositions look reasonable enough. They justify the actions of leaders and the sacrifices leaders demand of others. But a different picture emerges for some who self-consciously question the common assumptions regarding crises and examine their origins and impacts. It then appears that the recurrence of crises is predictable because they flow from inequalities in economic and political power; that the burdens of almost all crises fall disproportionately on the poor, while the influential and the affluent often benefit from them; and that they are closely linked to the social problems we define as normal.

This alternative set of beliefs about crises is put forward as a counterpoint to the conventional assumptions, and the challenge is ambivalently accepted. The two sets of cognitions comprise contradictory mythic explanations of crises, in the same way that there are contradictory myths about chronic social problems, and with the same political result: the ability to tolerate personal doubts and yet maintain integrity by turning to one or the other explanation as the need arises; general willingness to accept sacrifices rather than resist; and an adequate, though changing and ambiguous, level of support for the regime that presents itself as coping with the crisis. The presence in our political culture of conflicting beliefs, some justifying leaders' handling of crises and others holding leaders responsible for the burdens they impose, permits both governmental regimes and the mass of citizens to live with chronic crisis and with themselves.

The Labeling of Crises

The word "crisis" connotes a threat or emergency people must face together. More powerfully, perhaps, than any other political term, it suggests a need for unity and for common sacrifice. Yet each crisis is uneven in its impact, typically bringing deprivations for many, especially those who are politically and economically weak, and often bringing benefits to some who have the resources to deal with the new situation. As is often the case with controversial political issues, the language conventionally used to describe a crisis helps people to adapt to it by evoking a problematic picture of the issue. Wars are always presented as responses to foreign threats, and the response involves disproportionate susceptibility to military drafts and disproportionate sacrifice of living standards for the poor. The energy crisis of the early seventies, portrayed as a consequence of foreign decisions and a worldwide increase in demand, produced a profit bonanza for oil companies[1] and steep price increases that imposed burdens in inverse ratio to ability to pay. Crises flowing from fears of internal threats to security, such as the McCarthy years of the fifties and the Palmer Raids after World War I, impose severe burdens on liberals, reformers, and radicals, while realizing many conservative objectives. Economic crises that take the form of depression or serious recession hurt a large part of the middle class but strike most damagingly at unskilled workers and those whose jobs are marginal. While political rhetoric evokes a belief in a critical threat to a common "national interest," the impacts of each crisis inevitably reflect internal conflicts of interests and inequality of sacrifice.

[1] See p. 96.

It is very likely our ambivalence about this fact that makes it politically necessary to accept each crisis as unique, unexpected, a blatant deviation from the usual state of affairs, though crisis is the norm, not the exception. The forms of crisis already mentioned have occupied most of the years since World War I, and there were many others as well. Besides recurring wars, recessions and depressions, and internal security scares, the years between 1920 and 1975 saw: Teapot Dome, the international fascist threat of the thirties, the cold war, the civil rights disturbances of the late fifties and sixties, the Bay of Pigs, the Cuban missile crisis, the political assassinations of the sixties, the urban riots, the environmental crisis, and Watergate—to name only a cross-section.

This impressive catalogue was neither a series of accidents nor the result of conspiracies. It was the response of rational people to opportunities to make use of their economic and political resources. Stock market traders took advantage of credit opportunities in the twenties, and oil companies of their control over supply, distribution, and international trade and tax arrangements in 1973. In the same way political, military, and law enforcement officials, who draw power and status benefits from popular fears of internal or external enemies, naturally perceive, fantasize, publicize, or exaggerate the threat from alleged enemies.

The long-term developments that make it possible for strategically located groups to precipitate a crisis, unintentionally or deliberately, are always complex and ambiguous. People who benefit from a crisis are easily able to explain it to themselves and to the mass public in terms that mask or minimize their own contributions and incentives, while highlighting outside threats and unexpected occurrences. The divergence between the symbolic import of crises and their material impact is basic to their popular acceptance.

Ambiguity about the nature and meaning of crises is concurrent with conflicting incentives to accept them as unpreventable and to suspect them as part of a political or economic power game. There is, accordingly, always a sense in which the labeling of a set of events as a crisis is arbitrary and problematic. Mass acceptance of the label is necessary even if the acceptance is ambivalent. Consider the conditions under which such acceptance comes about. Many crises are precipitated by an event that rather suddenly makes clear the serious consequences of activities that have been going on for a long time without occasioning much concern. Limitations on refining capacity and long-standing tax and price arrangements among American oil companies and Middle East oil-producing countries set the stage for an energy crisis long before the sudden declaration in 1973 that oil was in short supply. Before every war there is a long sequence of incidents, tensions, and psychological influences upon public opinion, to which a declaration of war or an outbreak of fighting gives new meaning. Before every economic recession there are banking, corporate, and industrial relations decisions that eventuate in production cuts, serious unemployment, and a label that calls public attention to a threatening situation, so that they retrospectively come to be seen as precursors of a crisis.

A second kind of crisis is precipitated when people who have passively suffered grievances for many years begin to resist collectively, and so define the situation as critical rather than acceptable. The civil rights protests of the late fifties and early sixties, the urban riots of the late sixties, the environmental crisis, and Watergate were all crises of this kind. In the case of Wategate the activities ultimately defined as a national threat were deliberately concealed. Urban ghettos and ecological damage were apparent enough for many decades to anyone who was interested, but few took much notice until the late sixties, when everyone began to notice.

A third form of national crisis is created semantically and self-consciously by groups who engender widespread anxiety about an alleged threat that may or may not be real. The Cuban missile crisis of 1962 and the "missile gap" of 1960 are pristine examples. History is filled with instances of governments publicizing and exaggerating allegedly threatening movements by potentially hostile countries. The Kennedy administration did not see the maintenance of American missiles in Turkey, a few miles from the borders of the Soviet Union, as creating a crisis, but chose to define Russian missiles in Cuba as an intolerable threat. Any regime that prides itself on crisis management is sure to find crises to manage, and crisis management is always available as a way to mobilize public support.

Even more common than the semantically created crisis is the semantically masked crisis. Many problems that impoverish or ruin millions of lives are not perceived as crises because we attach labels and "explanations" to them that portray them as natural and inevitable, or as caused by the people who suffer from them rather than by outside, unexpected threats. We see poverty, crime, sickness, emotional disturbance, carnage on the highways, and similar disasters as chronic social "problems" rather than as crises, though they hurt more people more severely than any of the crises do. Those who suffer from problems that are never solved typically accept the prevailing view, including a demeaning conception of themselves, rather than seeing their problems as crises calling for drastic and resolute national action.

The various crises are sometimes closely linked to one another, even though each crisis is experienced as unique as it comes upon us. Internal security scares are predictable after major wars; the anxieties of the last war and anticipation of future ones engender fears of internal enemies and often justify austerity budgets, hard work, and low pay as well. The onset of a new crisis often saves some groups from the effects of a previous one. The energy crisis dramatically weakened the curbs on corporations stemming from the environmental crisis. Wars frequently end economic depressions and recessions.

Past crises become symbols whose meanings affect later developments. It is said that Richard Nixon saw Kennedy's handling of the Cuban missile crisis as the epitome of great national leadership and that he more easily decided on the secret bombing of Cambodia in 1969 and the Christmas bombing of Hanoi in 1972 because he equated those actions with Kennedy's heroic risk-taking respecting Cuba. The Great Depression of the thirties has repeatedly been used both to arouse suspicion of governmental intervention in economic affairs and to arouse suspicion of governmental passivity.

The lesson of all this is fundamental for understanding both the wide discretion enjoyed by governmental regimes and the willingness to tolerate that discretion while continuing to believe in popular sovereignty and the rule of law. Because the contradiction is built into our accepted modes of seeing and explaining public affairs, we rarely notice that it *is* a contradiction. Whether precipitated semantically or by some group's seizure of an opportunity for enhanced income or power, each crisis is perceived as unique and as reason for accepting special sacrifices. At the same time we look forward to a return to a state of affairs in which the normal rights of citizens and the normal restraints on governmental discretion will again prevail, hopefully forever after. In the meantime the belief in a crisis relaxes resistance to governmental interferences with civil liberties and bolsters support for executive actions, including discouragement or suppression of criticism and governmental failure to respond to it.

The recurrence of crises is bound to encourage less critical acceptance of governmental actions that would otherwise be resisted. That the various crises are of different kinds, intermingled with one another in what seems to be a random fashion, manifestly bolsters their psychological impact and makes it easier to perceive them as temporary and unavoidable departures from a "norm" of popular control over governmental discretion that in fact rarely exists.

While the perception of a crisis largely depends upon governmental cueing, the cueing is patterned, not random. Incumbent political regimes consistently minimize social and economic problems but are alarmist about threats to security, whether from abroad or from internal enemies and deviant people. Both these courses of action flow from political temptations that are always present. Every administration finds it politically useful to claim that its economic and social policies are working: that a monthly rise in unemployment or prices is an aberration, not a long-term trend; that "next year will be a very good year," for popular concern about these issues means votes against incumbents. Alarm about external or internal enemies, by contrast, makes people eager for resolute action and willing to entrust wider powers to leaders so that they can act effectively. There is, accordingly, a systematic deflation in governmental rhetoric of the developments that call attention to unequal distribution of goods and services and a systematic inflation of the forms of threat that legitimize and expand authority. The latter are defined as crises, the former as problems. As crises recur and problems persist, so does a governmental dramaturgy of coping.

Public Opinion

Any reference to "public opinion" calls to mind popular beliefs that influence public officials and inhibit politicians who try to oppose it. But there are conflicting opinions whenever there is an issue, by definition, and opinions shift with the social situation in which people find themselves, the information they get, and the level of abstraction at which the issue is discussed. There can be no one "public opinion" but, rather, many publics. Some opinions change easily, while others persist indefinitely.

To define beliefs as public opinion is itself a way of creating opinion, for such a reference both defines the norm that should be democratically supported and reassures anxious people that authorities respond to popular views. In short, "public opinion" is a symbol whether or not it is a fact. It is often nonexistent, even respecting important questions. Most of the population can have no opinion regarding thousands of technical, economic, professional, military, and other decisions. Pressure groups and government officials can usually cite public opinion as a reason for taking or avoiding action with confidence that they will not be proven wrong. If they define the public will at a high enough level of generality, they cannot be wrong.

Their own statements and actions, moreover, help generate the opinions on which they rely for support. Whenever a welfare administrator justifies the paring of welfare rolls on the ground that the public demands the elimination of chiselers, his statement triggers anxiety about fraud and laxity. Opinion polls help create the opinions they count when they incorporate evocative terms in their questions, as is inevitable if the questions deal with controversial matters.[2] In common with words like "democracy" and "justice," statements about "public opinion" help marshal support for particular policies. The term connotes a force independent of government, but a large part of it echoes the beliefs authorities deliberately or unconsciously engender by appealing to fears or hopes that are always prevalent, including suspicions of the poor and the unconventional.

Some people hold fairly stable opinions on issues that directly influence their public esteem and income. It is not chance that generals seldom advocate unilateral disarmament, that workers want high wages, or that college professors usually look with more favor on academic freedom than FBI agents do. This is a different phenomenon from the mass reactions to changing information and situations discussed in the last paragraph; but the term "public opinion" is applied to both of them and so confuses their separate functions. Authorities and pressure groups, like everyone else, can define, and so perceive, any belief as a parochial reflection of a narrow private interest, as held by the population generally, as transitory, or as stable, whichever of these categories suits their current interests. As a result, it is all the easier for public officials credibly to assert that

[2] Lee Bogart, *Silent Politics: Polls and the Awareness of Public Opinion* (New York: Wiley Interscience, 1972), pp. 99–140.

they are responding to opinion when they have created it; or to believe that a group they oppose is advancing its own narrow interests when that is the picture political adversaries always present to their opponents.

"Public opinion," then, is an evocative concept through which authorities and pressure groups categorize beliefs in a way that marshals support or opposition to their interests, usually unselfconsciously. Public opinion is not an independent entity, though the assumption that opinions spring autonomously into people's minds legitimizes the actions of all who can spread their own definitions of problematic events to a wider public.

A public administrative organization comes into being to reflect a particular body of opinion. The agencies that last represent a continuing interest that wields some political clout.[3] The Bureau of Indian Affairs, for example, represents the local groups with a continuing interest in controlling the social and economic activities of Indians more consistently than it reflects the diffuse liberal concern that Indians be protected and their problems ameliorated. An administrator or executive tries to survive by taking account of the conflicting interests that swirl around his policy area. Sometimes one or more of these interests is well-organized and damaging if resisted. Often there is a widely shared interest, like that of consumers, that is readily appeased through symbolic reassurance. And there are occasional waves of strong sentiment, such as ideological witch-hunts and revelations of official corruption, that sweep through large groups of people, but subside after a few months or a few years.

In these sometimes troubled waters, a public official is not a helpless boat at the mercy of currents and passing storms, for officials help stir up the currents that move them. In all the ways that authorities have at their disposal to build cognitive structures, officials shape mass opinion and only then reflect it, even while the socialization of citizens into the belief that executives and administrators exist to carry out the will of the people maintains a modicum of public support. Organized groups with political resources must be appeased; mass beliefs can be created, even if unintentionally.

Administrators categorize public issues so as to further the inter-

[3] Cf. Herbert A. Simon, "Birth of an Organization: The Economic Cooperation Administration," *Public Administration Review* 13 (Autumn 1953), pp. 227–38.

ests of the groups that gave birth to their agencies and that serve as their continuing patrons. They often define one controversial view as "public opinion" and so dismiss others as trivial or nonexistent. The school administrator who encourages teachers to offer bland courses and reading assignments so as not to offend "public opinion" is classifying one segment of opinion, usually a parochial one, as the universe; but it *is* likely to be the most vociferous view, the one that safeguards influential local interests, and it may be the opinion the administrator personally finds most congenial. To respond to it is certainly his or her least risky course. Such problematic categorization is typically not noticed or criticized, for it is defined as professionalism; while the occasional teacher who offends conservative opinion by introducing students to controversial views or information is likely to be noticed, brought into line, or dismissed.

In the same way, the mental health professionals routinely cite popular fears of the mentally ill and bias against them as a reason they must exercise strict controls over doubtful cases. Yet studies of opinion on this issue repeatedly show that in taking this view the professionals are influencing the attitudes of the general public rather than reflecting it. "A number of major studies have found society to be understanding and sympathetic toward its mentally ill members." [4] Several studies have found laymen defining many behaviors as normal that professionals defined as pathological.[5]

This research doubtless oversimplifies. Few laymen are likely to have clear and consistent opinions; but latent popular fears of pathology, illness, and inadequacy are certainly incited and reinforced by the warnings and categorizations of the helping professionals; they coexist with the recognition that children can be defined as deviant or backward when they behave and speak in school in ways that are normal at home, especially if "home" is a working-class or slum neighborhood.

For administrators the least risky strategy is so clear and so bene-

[4] Herzl R. Spiro et al., "Who's Kidding Whom," *Mental Hygiene* 56 (Spring 1972): 36–38.

[5] Elaine Cumming and John Cumming, *Closed Ranks* (Cambridge, Mass.: Harvard University Press, 1957), pp. 68–69. For a bibliography of other studies and a summary of their findings, see H. R. Spiro, I. Stassi, and G. Crocetti, "Ability of the Public to Recognize Mental Illness: An Issue of Substance and an Issue of Meaning," *Social Psychiatry* 8 (February 1973): 32–36.

ficial to themselves that they doubtless see it as rationality rather than strategy. The stable interests of the middle class are "public opinion," for the respectable can hurt recalcitrant officials. The interests of the poor and the insecure should be defined by experts and professionals who know what is best for them; for in spite of their large numbers they can be inadequate, and are typically sanctionless, ambivalent, and controllable. "Public opinion" regarding normality, competence, and deviance usually becomes what legitimate authority defines it to be, and that definition in turn becomes a self-fulfilling prophecy, while "professionalism" complements the process by rationalizing the regulation of the unconventional and the poor.

The selective perception of public opinion has practical consequences. Because the middle class demands it, "relief agencies are . . . compelled to invent rituals of degradation and to subject their clientele to them," say Piven and Cloward, referring to requirements that relief recipients and their children answer questions about their personal habits, sexual practices, and housekeeping routines.[6] Clients have sometimes been deterred by threats from their caseworkers from participating in civil rights protests, complaining about discrimination in housing, employment, or education, and even from voting in ways that displeased the agency.[7]

Schoolteachers and counselors also usually perceive merit in terms of conformity to middle-class opinion and norms. In a school studied by Cicourel and Kitsuse, all but three of fifteen students from the upper middle class were classified as "excellent" in achievement. But in assessing achievement the counselor subtly took account of other matters:

> Belonging to the "in-group" may be given greater weight than grade-point average in classifying a student as an "excellent student," or "getting into a lot of trouble" may be more important than "performing up to ability level" in deciding that a student is an "under-achiever."[8]

[6] Frances F. Piven and Richard A. Cloward, *Regulating the Poor* (New York: Vintage, 1971), p. 166.

[7] *Report of the United States Commission on Civil Rights*, Appendix I, quoted in Piven and Cloward, *Regulating the Poor*, p. 168.

[8] Aaron Cicourel and John I. Kitsuse, *The Educational Decision-Makers* (Indianapolis: Bobbs-Merrill, 1963), p. 71.

The same form of influence of social class upon perception holds for authorities responsible for prosecuting crime:

> This prejudice in favor of "our own kind" can be seen at its most blatant in the suggestion made in standard reference works on criminal procedure that prosecutors wisely refrain from prosecuting in cases of law violation where the offender comes from a "respectable background." [9]

In short, officials and public administrators are likely to perceive either as "public opinion" or as "professionalism" those opinions that they share personally or that can hurt their organizations. Few concepts are more ambiguous or more potent in shaping public policy than these two. Together, they enable officials to merge and confuse pride in doing competent work, class biases, concern for their own status, and fears about an adequate budget and to express them in terms that marshal wide support. "Public opinion" and "professionalism" perform all the functions of political condensation symbols. A class-based bias in policy appears in many different public organizations; but the subtly expressed posture of responsiveness to the public will and of a monopoly of specialized knowledge minimize criticism based on anxiety about bureaucratic arbitrariness and about the social problems with which the agencies deal.

The divisions in interests, fears, and hopes that permeate society also win a great deal of discretion and diffuse support for authorities. When officials define some people as dangerous, undeserving, or inadequate, they gain the support of all who share this view or who need a scapegoat to rationalize their own failings or guilt. The beneficiaries of existing economic and social institutions need to be assured that those institutions are sound, that their own success reflects merit, and that the failures have chiefly themselves to blame. People who are hurt by some public policies typically support the government in other areas and are ambivalent even about the acts that hurt them. The overall result is almost always a large net balance of support. The evocation of beliefs that encourage competition and distrust is a classic political recourse, though condensation symbolism usually prevents it from becoming a conscious strategy or from being perceived as one.

[9] American Friends Service Committee, *Struggle for Justice* (New York: Hill and Wang, 1971), p. 107.

Clearly, "public opinion" does have consequences, but rarely of the kind that promote the interests of the poor in a substantial way; for the term refers to a method of influencing popular demands, not necessarily of reflecting them. Rather than curbing a regime, "public opinion" as a symbol enlarges official discretion by immobilizing potential opposition.

The Political Language
of the Helping Professions

Hospital staff often deny or ignore the requests of angry mental patients because to grant them would "reinforce deviant behavior." Teachers sometimes use the same rationale to justify ignoring or punishing demanding students. Two recent presidents of the United States declared that they would pay no attention to peace demonstrators who resort to irritating methods. We commonly regard the last as a political act and the first two as therapeutic; but whether any such action is taken to be political or therapeutic depends on the assumptions of the observer, not on the behavior he or she is judging. Some psychologists reject the "reinforcement of deviant behavior" rationale on the ground that it pays no attention to the distinctive cognitive and symbolizing abilities of the human mind, equating people with rats. They believe such treatment too easily ignores reasonable grounds for anger and depresses the self-esteem of people who already suffer from too little of it, contributing to further "devi-

This chapter is a revised version of Murray Edelman, "The Political Language of the Helping Professions," *Politics and Society* 4 (Fall 1974): 295–310. © 1975 Geron–X, Inc.

ance," not to health. In this view the "treatment" is self-serving political repression, even if its definition as rehabilitation salves the consciences of professionals and of the public. Some psychiatrists, on the other hand, see political demonstrators or ghetto rioters as sick, calling for drugs or psychosurgery, not political negotiation, as the appropriate response; the Law Enforcement Assistance Administration has generously supported experiments based on that premise.

The language of "reinforcement" and "help" evokes a world in which the weak and the wayward need to be controlled for their own good. The language of "authority" and "repression" evokes a different reality, in which the rights of the powerless need to be protected against abuse by the powerful. Each linguistic form marshals public support for professional and governmental practices that have profound political consequences: for the status, the rights, and the freedom of professionals, of clients, and of the wider public as well; but we rarely have occasion to inhabit or examine both worlds at the same time.

Language is the distinctive characteristic of human beings. Without it we could not symbolize; we could not reason, remember, anticipate, rationalize, distort, and evoke beliefs and perceptions about matters not immediately before us. With it we not only describe reality but create our own realities, which take forms that overlap with one another and may not be mutually consistent. When it suits us to see rationalization as reason, repression as help, distortion as creation, or the converse of any of these, language and mind can smoothly structure each other to do so. When it suits us to solve complicated problems of logic and mathematics, language and mind can smoothly structure each other to do that as well. When the complicated problems involve social power and status, problematic perception and distortion are certain.

It is a commonplace of linguistic theory that language, thought, and action shape one another. Language is always an intrinsic part of some particular social situation; it is never an independent instrument or simply a tool for description. By naively perceiving it as a tool, we mask its profound part in creating social relationships and in evoking the roles and the "selves" of those involved in the relationships.

Because the helping professions define other people's statuses (and their own), the terms they employ to categorize clients and justify restrictions of their physical movements and of their moral and intellectual influence are especially revealing of the political functions language performs and of the multiple realities it helps create. Just as any single numeral evokes the whole number scheme in our minds, so a professional term, a syntactic form, or a metaphor with scientific connotations can justify a hierarchy of power for the person who uses it and for the groups that respond to it.

In analyzing such political evocations I do not mean to suggest that the helping professions cannot be rehabilitative and educational as well. Psychological distress can be as "real" as economic distress, and psychological support is often helpful for people who voluntarily seek it. There is a large literature and a complicated controversy about the links among psychological, economic, and social stress and about the effectiveness of the helping professions in achieving their goals; but this discussion focuses on the *political* consequences of professional language.

Through devices I explore here, the helping professions create and reinforce popular beliefs about which kinds of people are worthy and which are unworthy; about who should be rewarded through governmental action and who controlled or subjected to discipline. Unexamined language and actions can help us understand more profoundly than legislative histories or administrative or judicial proceedings how we decide upon status, rewards, and controls for the wealthy, the poor, women, conformists, and nonconformists.

In this chapter I examine such political uses of language in psychiatry, social work, psychiatric nursing, public school education, and law enforcement. My observations are based on extensive (and depressing) reading in the textbooks and professional journals of these professions. I looked for covert as well as overt justifications for status differentials, power differentials, and authority.

Therapy and Power

To illustrate the subtle bearing of language on status and authority consider a common usage that staff, clients, and the general public all accept as descriptive of a purely professional process: the term "therapy." In the journals, textbooks, and talk of the helping professions, the term is repeatedly used as a suffix or qualifier. Mental patients do not hold dances; they have dance therapy. If they play volleyball, that is recreation therapy. If they engage in a group discussion, that is group therapy.

Even reading is "bibliotherapy"; and the professional literature warns that it may be advisable to restrict, supervise, or forbid reading on some subjects, especially politics and psychiatry. Such an assertion forces us to notice what we normally pass over. To label a common activity as though it were a medical one is to establish superior and subordinate roles, to make it clear who gives orders and who takes them, and to justify in advance the inhibitions placed upon the subordinate class. It ordinarily does so without arousing resentment or resistance either in the subordinates or in outsiders sympathetic to them, for it superimposes a political relationship on a medical one while still depicting it as medical.

Though the linguistic evocation of the political system is subtle, that very fact frees the participants to act out their political roles blatantly, for they see themselves as helping, not as repressing. In consequence, assaults on people's freedom and dignity can be as polar and degrading as those typically occurring in authoritarian regimes, without qualms or protest by authorities, clients, or the public that hears about them. In this way a suffix or qualifier evokes a full-blown political system. No doubt it does so for most of the professionals who draw power from the system as persuasively and unobtrusively as it does for the clientele groups whom it helps induce to submit to authority and to accept the status of a person who must let others decide how he or she should behave.

To call explicit attention to the political connotations of a term for power, on the other hand, is to rally opposition rather than support. To label an authority relationship "tyrannical" is an exhortation to oppose it, not a simple description. The chief function of any political term is to marshal public support or opposition. Some terms do so overtly; but the more potent ones, including those used by professionals, do so covertly, portraying a power relationship as a helping one. When the power of professionals over other people is at stake, the language employed implies that the professional has ways to ascertain who are dangerous, sick, or inadequate; that he or she knows how to render them harmless, rehabilitate them, or both; and that the procedures for diagnosis and for treatment are too specialized for the lay public to understand or judge them. A patient with a sore throat is anxious for his doctor to exercise a certain amount of authority; but the diagnosis is easily checked, and the problem itself circumscribes the doctor's authority. When there is an allegation of mental illness, delinquency, or intellectual incapacity, neither the diagnosis nor the scope of authority is readily checked or limited, but its legitimacy is linguistically created and reinforced.

It is, of course, the ambiguity in the relationship, and the ambivalence in the professional and in the client, that gives the linguistic usage its flexibility and potency. That is always true of symbolic evocations, and it radically distinguishes such evocations from simple deception. Many clients want help, virtually all professionals think they are providing it, and sometimes they do so. Just as the helping seems manifest until it is self-consciously questioned, and then it becomes problematic, so the political relationship seems nonexistent until it is self-consciously questioned, and then it becomes manifest.

The special language of the helping professions merges cognition and affect. The term "mental illness" and the names for specific deviant behaviors encourage the observer and the actor to condense and confound several facets of his or her perception: helping the suffering, controlling the dangerous, sympathy for the former, fear of the latter, and so on. The terms carry all these connotations, and the actor-speaker-listener patterns them so as to utilize semantic ambiguity to cope with his or her ambivalence.

We normally fail to recognize this catalytic capacity of language because we think of linguistic terms and syntactical structures as signals rather than as symbols. If a word is a name for a specific thing or action, then terms like "mental illness," "delinquency prone," or "schizophrenic" have narrowly circumscribed meanings. But if a word is a symbol that condenses and rearranges feelings, memories, perceptions, beliefs, and expectations, then it evokes a particular structuring of beliefs and emotions, a structuring that varies with people's social situations. Language as symbol catalyzes a subjective world in which uncertainties and appropriate courses of action are clarified. Yet this impressive process of symbolic creation is not self-conscious. Our naive view holds that linguistic terms stand for particular objects or behavior, and so we do not ordinarily recognize that elaborate cognitive structures are built upon them.

In the symbolic worlds evoked by the language of the helping professions, speculation and verified fact readily merge with each other. Language dispels the uncertainty in speculation, changes facts to make them serve status distinctions, and reinforces ideology. The names for forms of mental illness, forms of delinquency, and for educational capacities are the basic terms. Each of them normally involves a high degree of unreliability in diagnosis, in prognosis, and in the prescriptions of rehabilitative treatments; but each also entails unambiguous constraints upon clients, especially their confinement and subjection to the staff and the rules of a prison, school, or hospital. The confinement and constraints are converted into liberating and altruistic acts by defining them as education, therapy, or rehabilitation and by other linguistic forms to be examined shortly. The arbitrariness and speculation in the diagnosis and the prognosis, on the other hand, are converted into clear and specific perceptions of the need for control. Regardless of the clinical utility of professional terms, their political utility is manifest; they marshal popular support for professional discretion, concentrating public attention upon procedures and rationalizing in advance any failures of the procedures to achieve their formal objectives.

Categorization is necessary to science and, indeed, to all perception. It is also a political tool, establishing status and power hierarchies. We ordinarily assume that a classification scheme is either scientific or political in character, but any category can serve either or both functions, depending on the interests of those who employ it rather than on anything inherent in the term. The name for a category therefore confuses the two functions, consigning people to high or low status and power while drawing legitimacy from its scientific status.

Any categorization scheme that consigns people to niches according to their actual or potential accomplishments or behavior is bound to be political, no matter what its scientific function. IQs; psychiatric labels; typologies of talent, skills, or knowledge; employment statuses; criminal statuses; personality types—all exemplify the point. Regardless of their validity and reliability (which are notoriously low) [1] or their analytic uses, such classifications rank people and determine degrees of status and of influence. The categorizations of the helping professions are pristine examples of the function, and many of these categories carry over into the wider society. Once

---

[1] See, for example, Lawrence G. Kolb, Viola Bernard, and Bruce P. Dohrenwend, "The Problem of Validity in Field Studies of Psychological Disorder," in *Challenges to Psychiatry*, ed. Bruce P. Dohrenwend and Barbara Snell Dohrenwend (New York: Wiley, 1969), pp. 429–60; Linda Burzotta Nilson and Murray Edelman, "The Symbolic Evocation of Occupational Prestige," University of Wisconsin—Madison, Institute for Research on Poverty, Discussion Paper 348–76.

established, a categorization defines what is relevant about the people who are labeled. It encourages others to interpret developments so as to confirm the label and to ignore, discount, or reinterpret counter-evidence. As a civil rights lawyer put it, "While psychiatrists get angry, patients get aggressive; nurses daydream, but patients withdraw." [2] The eternal human search for meaning and for status can be counted on to fuel the problematic interpretation.

The language of the helping professions reveals in an especially stark way that perception of the same act can range all the way from one pole to its opposite. Is an action punishment or is it help? The textbooks and psychiatric journals recommend actions that look like sadism to many and like therapy to many others: deprivation of food, bed, walks in the open air, visitors, mail, and telephone calls; solitary confinement; deprivation of reading and entertainment materials; immobilizing people by tying them into wet sheets and then exhibiting them to staff and other patients; other physical restraints on body movement; drugging the mind against the client's will; incarceration in locked wards; a range of public humiliations such as the prominent posting of alleged intentions to escape or commit suicide, the requirement of public confessions of misconduct or guilt, and public announcement of individual misdeeds and abnormalities.

The major psychiatric and nursing journals describe and prescribe all these practices, and more repressive ones, repeatedly. The May 1973 issue of *Psychiatry* tells of a psychiatric ward in which, as a part of her therapy, a sobbing patient was required to scrub a shower room floor repeatedly with a toothbrush while two "psychiatric technicians" stood over her shouting directions, calling her stupid, and pouring dirty water on the floor.[3] Another professional article suggests withholding meals from noncompliant patients,[4] and a third recommends that cold wet sheet pack restraints be used more often, because they gratify the patient's dependency needs.[5]

[2] Daniel Oran, "Judges and Psychiatrists Lock Up Too Many People," *Psychology Today* 7 (August 1973): 22.

[3] D. L. Staunard, "Ideological Conflict on a Psychiatric Ward," *Psychiatry* 36 (May 1973): 143–56.

[4] Carl G. Carlson, Michael Hersen, and Richard M. Eisler, "Token Economy Programs in the Treatment of Hospitalized Adult Psychiatric Patients," *Mental Health Digest* 4 (December 1972): 21–27.

[5] Rose K. Kilgalen, "Hydrotherapy—Is It All Washed Up?" *Journal of Psychiatric Nursing* 10 (November–December 1972): 3–7.

Public humiliation and pain, even when employed only occasionally and perceived as therapy, have systematic effects on people who know they may experience them and on those who use them. In the institutions run by the helping professions, the threat of their use helps keep inmates docile. Ivan Illich remarks of such "random terror" that it serves to "break the integrity of an entire population and make it plastic material for the teaching invented by technocrats," [6] a lesson despotic governments have always been quick to learn.

The outsider acting as critic or skeptic is likely to perceive professional actions in this way, while the insider does not do so while playing the expected professional role. Yet there is ambivalence; and it is one of the functions of professional language and professional journals to help resolve it by defining constraints as help. The *Journal of Psychiatric Nursing*, for example, rarely fails to publish at least one article in each issue that encourages nurses to overcome their qualms about denying patients the rights other people enjoy; the question is presented as a search for therapy, never as a search for autonomy, dignity, or civil rights.

To describe these practices in everyday language evokes shock at the "treatments" in a person who takes the description naively, without the conditioning to the professional perspective to which everyone has in some degree been exposed. In the professionals and those who accept their perspective, on the other hand, it is the *language* rather than the actions that evokes horror, for they have been socialized to see these things only as procedures, as *means* to achieve rehabilitation, not as constraints upon human beings. Language is consequently perceived as a distortion if it focuses on immediate impacts on clients rather than on the ultimate ends that the professional thinks the client should read into them and that the professional himself or herself reads into them.

The professional's reaction to language of this kind exemplifies the reaction of powerful people in general to accounts of their dealings with those over whom they hold authority. Because the necessary condition of willing submission to authority is a belief that submission benefits the subordinate, it is crucial to the powerful that descriptions of their treatment of others highlight the benefit and not the physical, psychological, or economic costs of submission. The

[6] Ivan Illich, *Deschooling Society* (New York: Harper and Row, 1971), p. 14.

revenue service deprives people of money, almost always involuntarily; the military draft imposes involuntary servitude; thousands
of other agents of the state deprive people of forms of freedom.
Usually the rationale for such restraints is an ambiguous abstraction:
national security, the public welfare, law and order. We do not
experience or name these ambiguous and abstract objectives as any
different from goals that consist of concrete benefits, such as traffic
control and disease control. Linguistic ambiguity spreads the rationale of these latter types of benefits to justify far more severe constraints and deprivations (including death in war) in policy areas
in which benefits are nondemonstrable and doubtless often nonexistent. We experience as radical rhetoric any factual description
of authoritative actions that does not call attention to their alleged
benefits to all citizens or to some, and authorities typically characterize such descriptions as subversive, radical, or treasonous. They
are indeed subversive of ready submission and of political support.

The point becomes vivid if we restate the actions described above
from the professional's perspective: discouraging sick behavior and
encouraging healthy behavior through the selective granting of rewards; the availability of seclusion, restraints, and closed wards to
grant a patient a respite from interaction with others and from making decisions, and to prevent harm to himself or others; enabling him
to think about his behavior, to cope with his temptations to "elope"
or succumb to depression, and to develop a sense of security; immobilizing the patient to calm him, satisfy his dependency needs,
give him the extra nursing attention he values, and enable him to
benefit from peer confrontation; placing limits on his acting out;
and teaching him that the staff cares.

The two accounts describe the same phenomena, but they occur in
phenomenologically different worlds. Notice that the professional
terms carry connotations that depict constraints as nonrestrictive. To
speak of "elopement" rather than "escape," as psychiatrists and staff
members do, is to evoke a picture of individual freedom to leave
when one likes (as eloping couples do) rather than of locks, iron
bars, and bureaucratic prohibitions against voluntary departure. To
speak of "seclusion" or "quiet room" rather than solitary confinement is again to suggest voluntary and enjoyable retirement from
others and to mask the fact that the patient is locked in against his
or her will and typically resists and resents the incarceration. Such
terms accomplish in a craftsmanlike and nonobvious way what pro-

fessionals also say explicitly to justify restrictions on inmates. They assert in textbooks, journals, and assurances to visitors that some patients feel more secure in locked wards and in locked rooms, that professionals know when this is the case, and that the patients' statements to the contrary cannot be taken at face value.

To speak of "limits" is to mask the perception of punishment for misbehavior and to perceive the patient as inherently irrational, thereby diverting attention from the manifest frustrations and aggravations that come from bureaucratic restrictions and from consignment to the most powerless status in the institution.

Many clients come, in time, to use the professionals' language and to adopt their perspective. To the staff, their adoption of the approved linguistic forms is evidence of insight and improvement. All clients probably do this in some degree, but for many the degree is so slight that the professional descriptions serve as irony or as mockery. They are repeatedly quoted ironically by students, patients, and prisoners.

In the institutions run by the helping professions, established roles and their special language create a world with its own imperatives. The phenomenon helps us understand the frequency with which well-meaning men and women support governments that mortify, harass, torture, and kill large numbers of their citizens. To the outsider such behavior signals sadism and self-serving evil, and it is impossible to identify with it. To the people who avidly act out their roles inside that special world, motives, actions, and consequences of acts are radically different. Theirs is a work of purification and nurturance: of ridding the inherently or ideologically contaminated of their blight or of ridding the world of the contamination they embody. It is no accident that repressive governments are consistently puritanical. To the inhabitants of other worlds the repression is a mask for power, but to those who wield authority, power is a means to serve the public good. Social scientists cannot explain such phenomena as long as they place the cause inside people's psyches rather than in the social evocation of roles. To attribute evil or merit to the psyche is a political act rather than a medical one, for it justifies repression or exaltation, while minimizing observation and analysis. To explore phenomenological diversity in people's worlds and roles is to begin to recognize the full range of politics.

Class or status differences may also entail wide differences in the labelings of identical behaviors. The teacher's underachiever may be the epitome of the "cool" student who refuses to "brownnose." The middle class's criminal or thief may be a "political prisoner" to the black poor. Such labels with contrasting connotations occur when a deprived population sees the system as unresponsive to its needs and organized rebellion as impossible. In these circumstances, only individual nonconformity remains as a way to maintain self-respect. To the deprived the nonconformity is a political act. To the beneficiaries of the system it is individual pathology. Each labels it accordingly.

The term "juvenile delinquent" historically served the political function of forcing the assimilation of Catholic immigrants to the WASP culture of late nineteenth- and early twentieth-century America. This new category defined as "criminal" youthful behaviors handled informally among the urban Catholics and not perceived by them as crime at all: staying out late, drinking, smoking, reading comic books, truancy, disobedience. However, the definition of prevailing urban norms as "delinquency" justified the authorities in getting the Irish children away from their "bigoted" advisers, the priests.[7] The language of individual pathology served also to raise doubts about a distinctive culture and a religion, rationalizing its political consequences in terms of its motivation of salvaging youth from crime.

Some professionals reject the professional perspective, and all, no doubt, retain some skepticism about it and some ability to see things from the perspective of the client and the lay public. The ambivalence is typically resolved in more militant, decisive, and institutionalized forms than is true of ambivalent clients; for status, self-conception, and perhaps income hinge on its resolution. In consequence, professionals adopt radical therapy, existentialist or Szaszian views, or they attack these dissidents as unprofessional and unscientific.

The lay public by and large adopts the professional perspective; for its major concern is to believe that others can be trusted to handle these problems, which are potentially threatening to them but not a part of their everyday lives. This public reaction is the politically crucial one, for it confers power upon professionals and spreads their norms to others. The public reaction, in turn, is a response to

[7] Anthony M. Platt, The Child Savers: The Invention of Delinquency (Chicago: University of Chicago Press, 1969); American Friends Service Committee, Struggle for Justice (New York: Hill and Wang, 1971), p. 112.

the language of the professionals and to the social milieu which gives that language its authoritative meaning.

The Formal Component in Professional Language

The formal component in professional language is always significant; it consists for the laymen of meanings evoked by the *style* of expression, as distinct from its denotative content: the connotations, for example, of unfamiliar or scientific-sounding terms and of references to an esoteric body of theory. For the professional, formality entails reacting to "symptoms" only in ways that are approved in the textbooks and professional journals. These responses may be unfamiliar to laymen; they constrain cognition within a limited range, excluding originality outside that range.[8] That a battered woman is probably masochistic is an approved response for the psychoanalytically oriented psychiatrist. That any former psychiatric patient is "cured" is not an approved response, suggesting naivete and an unprofessional stance. The accepted word is "improved"; it justifies continued surveillance and control.

Both professionals and laymen, then, respond partly to the *forms* of language, as predetermined by the categories and observational methods of the profession. These forms evoke perceptions and beliefs that are all the more potent because they are subtly and often unconsciously expressed and understood. They mark off the insiders from the outsiders and they reinforce the willingness of the client to accept authority. Through ambiguous language forms, professionals, clients, and outsiders manage to adjust to one another and to themselves and to establish and maintain hierarchies of authority and status.

Professional Imperialism

The special language of the helping professions extends and enlarges authority as well as defining and maintaining it. It does so by

[8] For a perceptive discussion of the functions of formality in political language, see Maurice Block, ed., *Political Language and Oratory in Traditional Society* (New York: Academic Press, 1975), pp. 1–28.

defining the deviance of one individual as necessarily involving others as well, by seeing the absence of deviant behaviors as evidence of incipient deviance, and by defining as deviant forms of behavior that laymen regard as normal.

Because man is a social animal, deviance by definition involves others as well. In the helping professions, this truism serves as a reason to multiply the range of people over whom the professional psychiatrist, school psychologist, social worker, and law enforcement officer exercises authority. The "multiproblem family" needs counseling or therapy as much as its emotionally disturbed member. The person who offends others needs help even if she or he does not want it; and the professional has an obligation to "reach out" or engage in "case finding." These phrases interpret the sense in which deviance is social in character in a particular way: namely, that because other people are involved, their states of mind need the ministrations of the professional. By the same token they mask an alternative view: that it is the conditions of deviants' lives, their environments, and their opportunities that primarily need change. The professional interpretation, whatever its clinical uses, also serves the political function of extending authority over those not yet subject to it and the more far-reaching political function of shaping public perceptions so as to divert attention from economic and social institutions.

The more sweeping professional forays into alien territory rely on lack of evidence to prove the need for treatment. Consider one of the favorite terms of social work literature: the "predelinquent"; and corresponding psychiatric terms, like the "prepsychotic." On their face, such terms imply that the reference is to all who have not yet misbehaved, and that is certainly one of their connotations, one that would appear to give the professional *carte blanche* to assert authority over everybody who has not yet committed a crime or displayed signs of disturbance.

Though they do justify a wide range of actions, the terms usually have a considerably narrower connotation in practice, for social workers, teachers, psychiatrists, and law enforcement officials apply them largely to the poor and usually to children. Affluent adults may be "predelinquent" or "prepsychotic"; but it is not behavior that governs the connotations of these terms, but, rather, the statistical chances for a group and the belief that poor children are high risks, especially if they come from broken homes. They are indeed high statistical risks: partly because their labeling as predelinquents and the extra surveillance are certain to yield a fair number of offenders, just as they would in a wealthy population, and partly because poverty does not encourage adherence to middle-class norms.

In a program to treat "predelinquents" in a middle-class neighborhood of Cambridge–Somerville, Massachusetts, the "treated" group more often became delinquent than a control group, due, apparently, to the effects on the labeled people of their stigmatization. In a similar experiment in a slum neighborhood this result did not appear, apparently because the stigmatization was not significantly different from the normal low self-concept of the people involved.[9]

The term "predelinquent" nonetheless focuses the mind of its user and of his or her audience on the utility of preventative surveillance and control and diverts attention from the link between poverty and delinquency. The term also evokes confidence in the professional's ability to distinguish those who will commit crimes in the future from those who will not. Once again we have an illustration of the power of an unobtrusive symbol to evoke a structured world and to direct perception and norms accordingly.

Still another form of extension of authority through the pessimistic interpretation of normal behavior is exemplified in the psychiatric phrase "escape to health." The term again draws its connotation from the disposition to interpret behavior according to the status of the person engaging in it. If a psychiatric patient shows no pathological symptoms, the professional can designate the phenomenon as "escape to health," implying that the healthy behavior is itself a sign that the patient is still sick, possibly worse than before, but intent now on deceiving himself and the staff. The consequence is continued control over him or her.

The term epitomizes an attitude common to authorities who know or suspect that their charges would prefer to escape their supervision rather than "behave themselves." The student typed as a troublemaker or as unreliable excites as much suspicion when he is quiet as when he is active. Parole boards have their choice of interpreting an inmate's conformist prison behavior as reform or as cunning

---

[9] Jackson Toby, "An Evaluation of Early Identification and Intensive Treatment Programs for Predelinquents," *Social Problems* 13 (Fall 1965): 160–75; David B. Harris, "On Differential Stigmatization for Predelinquents," *Social Problems* 15 (Spring 1968): 507–8.

deception. Anxious public officials in all historical eras have feared both passivity and peaceful demonstrations among the discontented as the groundwork for rebellion. Always, there are metaphoric phrases to focus such anxieties and arouse them in the general public: underground subversion, plotting, the calm before the storm, quiet desperation, escape to health. Always, they point to an internal psychological state or an allegation not susceptible to observation.

In the schools, other phrases emphasize student nonactions, discount their observable actions, and so justify special staff controls over them. Especially common are "underachiever" and "overachiever." The former implies that the student is lazy, the latter that he or she is neurotic. "Overachiever" is an especially revealing case, for it offers a rationale for treating achievement as deviance. The helping professions are often suspicious of people who display talents beyond the "norm," as they must be in view of their veiled equation of the norm with health. Textbooks in "special education" and "learning disabilities" group gifted or exceptionally able students with the retarded and the emotionally disturbed as special students and advocate separating these "special" students from the normal ones. They urge that the gifted be required to do extra work ("enrichment"). This may or may not mean they learn more or learn faster. It certainly means that they are kept busy and so discouraged either from making demands on the teacher's time or intelligence or from pointing up the stultifying character of the curriculum through restiveness or rebelliousness.

At least as common is the view that the poor require treatment and control whether or not they display any pathological symptoms. Though this belief is manifestly political and class based, the language social workers use to justify surveillance and regulation of the poor is psychological in character. Here are some examples from social work and psychiatric journals and textbooks.

Regarding a preschool nursery in a slum area:

> The children did not have any diagnosed pathology, but as a result of existing in an atmosphere of cultural deprivation, they were vulnerable to many psychosocial problems.[10]

[10] Evelyn McElroy and Anita Narcisco, "Clinical Specialist in the Community Mental Health Program," *Journal of Psychiatric Nursing* 9 (January–February 1971): 19.

From an article in *Social Work* suggesting devices through which a social caseworker can induce the poor to come for counseling or treatment by deceiving them into thinking they are only accompanying their children, or only attending a party or social meeting:

> cognitive deficiency . . . broadly refers to the lacks many people suffer in the normal development of their thinking processes. For the most part, though not exclusively, such deficits occur among the poor regardless of nationality or race.[11]

The same article quotes a memorandum issued by the Family Service Association of Nassau County: "Culturally deprived adults seem to be impaired in concepts of causality and time." [12] This last sentence very likely means that the poor are likely to attribute their poverty to inadequate pay or unemployment rather than to personal defects (causality) and are not punctual in keeping appointments with caseworkers (time). It is bound to be based on a limited set of observations that have powerful implications for the professional observer's own status and authority. The quotation is an example of one of the most common linguistic devices for connoting pathology from specific behaviors equally open to alternative interpretations that make them seem normal. One of several concrete acts becomes a generalization about an "impairment." To those who do not know the basis for the generalization, it is *prima facie* scientific. To the professionals who have already been socialized into the view the generalization connotes, it is persuasive and profound. To those who meet neither of these conditions, it is a political exhortation rather than a scientific generalization; these people are inclined to treat it as problematic and controversial rather than as established by authoritative procedures.

Ambiguous language can also be vacuous, making it easy for professionals to legitimize social and political biases. They are not prejudiced against the poor, but against cognitive deficiencies; not

---

[11] Robert Sunley, "New Dimensions in Reaching-out Casework," *Social Work* 13 (April 1968): 64–74. For evidence that psychiatrists diagnose poorer patients as having more severe pathologies, see Joel Fischer, "Negroes and Whites and Rates of Mental Illness," *Psychiatry* 32 (November 1969): 428–46. See also Vernon L. Allen, "Personality Correlates of Poverty," in *Psychological Factors in Poverty*, ed. Vernon Allen (Chicago: Markham, 1970), pp. 242–66.

[12] Ibid., p. 73.

against women, but against impulsive-hysterics; not against political radicals, but against paranoids; not against homosexuals, but against deviants. They are not in favor of punishing, stigmatizing, humiliating, or imprisoning people but, rather, of meeting dependency and security needs, and of rehabilitation.

It is not chance that the groups constrained by these rationales are also the groups that experience bias in society at large or that the "treatment" consists either of restoring conformist behavior or of removing offenders from the sight, the consciences, and the career competition of the conventional. Those who become clients have experienced problems either because they have acted unconventionally or because they belong to a category (the young, the poor, women, blacks) whose behavior is largely assessed because of who they are rather than because of what they do.

"Helping" as a Political Symbol

The ambiguity of "helping" is apparent when we examine the contrasting ways in which society "helps" elites and nonelites. Subsidies from the public treasury to businessmen are justified not as help to individuals but as promotion of a popularly supported goal: defense, agriculture, transportation, and so on. The abstractions are not personified in the people who get generous depletion allowances, cost-plus contracts, tax write-offs, or free government services. To perceive the expenditure as a subsidy to real people would portray it as an inequity in public policy. The word "help" is not used in this context, though these policies make people rich and substantially augment the wealth of the already rich. Nor is there a dependency relationship or a direct personal relationship between a recipient and a grantor with discretion to withhold benefits. The grantor wields no power over the recipient; if anything, the recipient wields power over the administrators who carry out the law; for there are always legislators and executives ready to penalize administrators who call attention to the subsidy aspect of the program; and some of the more cooperative administrators can look forward to employment in the industries they come to know as dispensers of governmental benefits.

When "help" is given to the poor or the unconventional, a different set of role relationships and benefits appears. Now it is the beneficiaries who are sharply personified and brought into focus. They are individuals living off the taxpayer or flouting conventionality. What they personify is poverty, delinquency, or other forms of deviance. They are in need of help, but help in money, in status, and in autonomy must be sharply limited so as to avoid malingering. One of the consistent characteristics of the "helping" institutions is their care to limit forms of help that would make clients autonomous: money for the poor; education and independence for children of the poor or for "criminals"; physical and intellectual autonomy. The limit is enforced in practice while often denied in rhetoric.

The "help" for nonelite recipients of the largesse of the state that draws ready political support is control of their deviant tendencies: laziness, mental illness, criminality, nonconformity. They are taught to tolerate indignity and powerlessness when employed, poverty when unemployed, and the family and social stresses flowing from these conditions, without unconventional modes of complaint or resistance and without making too many demands on society.

In at least one of the worlds elites and professionals create for themselves and for a wider public, the help is real and the need for it is manifest. So manifest that it must be given even if it is not wanted. So manifest that failure to want it becomes evidence that it is needed and that it should be forced on recipients involuntarily and through incarceration if necessary.

When a helping relationship of this kind is established, it is likely to dominate the self-conception and the world view of those on both sides of the relationship. When a doctor sets a patient's broken arm, neither doctor nor patient lets the relationship significantly influence their self-conceptions or their views of their functions in society. When a public official tests an applicant for a driver's license or a radio license, this relationship is also just one more among many for both parties. But the psychiatrist who defines a patient as psychopathic or paranoid, or the teacher who defines a student as a slow learner or a genius, creates a relationship that is far more fundamental and influential for both professional and client. It tells them both who they are and so fundamentally creates their social worlds that they resist evidence that the professional competence of the one or the stigmatizing or exalting label of the other may be unwarranted. For both, the label tends to become a self-fulfilling prophecy and sometimes immune to falsifying evidence.

In consequence, the professional and the public official whose function it is to "help" the inadequate, the powerless, or the deviant is willing and eager to play his or her role, equipped with a built-in reason to discount or reinterpret qualms, role conflicts, and disturbing facts. To comfort, to subsidize, to limit, to repress, to imprison, even to kill are all sometimes necessary to protect the client and society, and the conscientious professional or political authority plays his role to be true to himself.

A society that frustrates or alienates a sizable proportion of its inhabitants can survive only as long as it is possible to keep the discontented docile and to isolate or incarcerate those who refuse to be "rehabilitated." The helping professions are the most effective contemporary agents of social conformity and isolation. In playing this political role they undergird the entire political structure, yet they are largely spared from self-criticism, from political criticism, and even from political observation, through a special symbolic language.

The Language of Bureaucracy

The largely unpublicized decisions of hundreds of thousands of people working in administrative organizations determine who gets what, but the news focuses on elections and on the pronouncements and decisions of executives, legislators, and high courts. The governmental activities that attract the widest public attention influence people's minds without otherwise directly affecting their lives. A declaration of war, to consider an extreme case, engenders a great many hopes, fears, and beliefs; but its impact on everyday life depends on the specific actions of draft boards, price and wage boards, production boards, and many other administrative bodies. A law or court decision guaranteeing equal rights means little in the life of a ghetto resident whose right to housing or fair employment is still not protected, though the news may reassure liberals.

Administrative agencies sometimes accomplish their objectives, and often they do not, but their survival or demise seems to depend on public anxiety about the problems with which they cope, not on their effectiveness in solving them. Their ineffectiveness when it occurs, and their public support whether or not it occurs, stem largely from language forms that help maintain anxiety but also interpret virtually *any* policy outcome as acceptable. Language shapes what administrators and the public take for granted, whose expectations they accept as legitimate and whose they ignore, how they define their functions, and what meanings they read into the outcomes of their policies. This chapter examines bureaucratic language of this kind. It is not the only form of language administrators use, or there would be no administrative accomplishments. But public administrative organizations are key instruments for influencing opinion through problematic language.

The only way governments can provide services to large numbers of people and control large populations is through organizations whose staff members are ranked in hierarchies of authority and assigned to perform distinctive functions. As we shall see, what are called "services" also act as controls, and what are defined as "controls" furnish valuable services to some. This ambiguity in definition and in perception is a major source of bureaucratic power and discretion, and it complements a related ambiguity as to when administrators solve and when they aggravate the problems with which they are supposed to cope.

Administrative organizations justify their discretionary powers on the ground that specialized knowledge, objectivity, and impersonality characterize bureaucracy.[1] In the light of the consequences of governmental administrative actions, each of these terms must be recognized as ambiguous, serving in practice to legitimize generous services and little regulation for some whose power is widely feared, and small services and major controls over larger numbers perceived as wielding little power. Terms have this consequence because bureaucratic language and actions respond to political sanctions, not because of any inherent bias in words or in administrators.

The Political Setting of Bureaucracy

The names of administrative organizations and of their subunits call attention to interests that are widely shared and that evoke broad support; they never adequately specify the groups to which an

---

[1] Cf. Max Weber, "Bureaucracy," in Robert K. Merton et al., *Reader in Bureaucracy* (Glencoe, Ill.: The Free Press, 1952).

organization has to respond in order to survive. The name of the Federal Communications Commission reflects everyone's need for communication services but masks the Commission's consistent sensitivity to the financial interests of the broadcasters and utilities it licenses.[2] Everyone needs food, but the Department of Agriculture has been notably more sensitive to the concerns of commercial farmers than to the nutritional needs of consumers or of the poor.[3]

A welfare department or education department bears a name that is even less adequate in defining the priorities to which it must respond. In the degree that people with influence in the community are serious about poverty and learning, these organizations reflect that concern. In the degree that influential people worry about laziness, unconventionality, or a large and docile labor supply, schools and welfare agencies respond to those concerns, which usually run counter to the elimination of poverty or the encouragement of learning.[4]

Organizations survive by reflecting the interests of those who can help or hurt them. At the same time, they mollify a wider public and immobilize potential opposition and internal qualms as well as they can through problematic definitions of what they do and equally problematic definitions of the public opinion to which they respond.

Administrative Ineffectiveness: Clear and Problematic

Though administrative organizations justify their powers and actions on the ground that they have specialized knowledge, they often continue indefinitely to pursue policies that are ineffective by widely accepted tests or that seem so to scholars and to many of their ostensible beneficiaries. Because of conflicting goals, ambiguous language, and the uncertain or mixed impact of administrative actions, assessments of the effectiveness of controversial organiza-

---

[2] Cf. Murray Edelman, *The Licensing of Radio Services in the United States, 1927 to 1947* (Urbana: University of Illinois Press, 1950).

[3] Cf. *New York Times*, 11 April 1972, p. 21; *New York Times*, editorial, 17 March 1975.

[4] For a discussion and documentation, see pp. 79–84.

tions typically tell more about the values of the observer than about policy consequences.

Administrative agencies that deal with poor, sick, wayward, or immature clients might be thought relatively immune from conflicting objectives, for help and rehabilitation draw little opposition as goals, in contrast, say, to the explicit conflict inherent in the work of agencies like the National Labor Relations Board or the price support function of the Department of Agriculture. Conflict or consensus about goals depends on the level of abstraction with which the goal is named in both kinds of organizations. When objectives and actions are specific, conflict appears; but public support for "help," "national security," "parity," "decent housing," or "a fair day's wage," is as readily forthcoming as it is meaningless. Evaluation of the achievement of vague objectives inevitably exaggerates results and the utility of services.

When organizational objectives are stated in concrete terms, many studies find them strikingly ineffective, though articles in the administrators' professional journals almost always see success. It is hard for anyone who reviews evaluations of organizational effectiveness to avoid the conclusion that what such studies "find" hinges upon how they define organizational goals and how they define the policy outcomes they assess. Definition, perception, and interpretation are crucial, for the same results mean very different things to different administrators and to outsiders who examine their policies.

Social work counseling, for example, apparently has little or no effect on client satisfaction, behavior, or the size of relief rolls. Even when offered under nearly ideal conditions (highly educated professionals and small, specially selected caseloads), clients look on the services as pleasant but irrelevant and caseloads do not decline as a result.[5] An experiment in a vocational high school found that a control group receiving no therapy showed no more continued delinquent behavior than a group getting intensive therapy.[6] In another experiment, with family therapy, a demonstration group improved by so slight a margin over a control group over a period of thirty-one months that the difference was not statistically signifi-

[5] Joel Handler and Ellen Jane Hollingsworth, The "Deserving Poor": A Study of Welfare Administration (New York: Academic Press, 1971), pp. 127–28.
[6] Henry J. Meyer, Edgar F. Borgatta, and Wyatt C. Jones, Work Intervention (New York: Russell Sage, 1965).

cant.[7] Between 1964 and 1970, social service expenditures increased from 100 million dollars to 600 million while welfare caseloads were growing from 7 to 13 million, suggesting to a leading student of the subject that social services to a low-income population do not reduce relief rolls.[8]

The treatment of criminals in prison is at least as ineffective and in many cases generates more crime, according to many studies. A recent one concludes that "there is considerable evidence that various treatment strategies do not make *any* significant difference in the future criminal behavior of inmates."[9] The length of prison sentences has been increasing, with median time served rising from twenty-four to thirty-six months between 1959 and 1969, while the number of persons imprisoned has also risen continuously and recidivism rates have remained about the same. About 40 percent of prisoners released on parole return within two to three years.[10] Another study puts it at between 35 and 55 percent, depending on the method of measurement.[11] Probationers have substantially lower rates of recidivism than those who are imprisoned, and inmates with shorter sentences have significantly lower rates than those with longer sentences.[12] Eysenck concluded from a review of the available studies that it makes no difference on the outcome what type of sentence an offender receives (from a warning through imprisonment), how soon he or she is released, how large a caseload the probation officer has, or whether the offender has received psychotherapy.[13]

Some research comparing people treated at suicide prevention centers with completed suicides concludes that the prevention centers have not lowered the suicide rate at all. People defined as suicidal

---

[7] Gordon E. Brown, ed., *The Multi-Problem Dilemma: A Social Research Demonstration with Multi-Problem Families* (Metuchen, N.J.: Scarecrow Press, 1968).

[8] Gilbert Y. Steiner, *The State of Welfare* (Washington, D.C.: The Brookings Institution, 1971), pp. 35–40.

[9] American Friends Service Committee, *Struggle for Justice* (New York: Hill and Wang, 1971), p. 87.

[10] Ibid., pp. 91–92.

[11] Martin A. Levin, "Crime, Punishment, and Social Science," *The Public Interest* (Spring 1972): 96.

[12] Ibid., p. 97.

[13] Hans J. Eysenck, *Crime and Personality* (London: Routledge and Kegan Paul, 1964), pp. 141–42.

at the centers differ in significant characteristics from people who take their lives, the latter being older, sicker, more successful, and less likely to come from broken homes.[14]

The claimed achievements of hospitals that offer treatment for emotional disturbance are subject to the greatest doubt. The *International Encyclopedia of the Social Sciences* sums up both the hopes and the evidence when it declares "There seems to be no widespread doubt that therapy is helpful, or at least that it is in some cases. But there is no satisfactory statistical evidence as yet that therapy benefits a population of patients." [15] Eysenck declares that the effectiveness claims seldom take account of spontaneous improvement without treatment.[16] The results of self-interest and problematic definition are also evident in the claims practitioners of each type of therapy make for their own theories and their disparagement of the claims of others. Professionals' ratings of patient improvement are greatly influenced by the patient's family's wishes and by his or her adaptation to expected hospital behavior and attitudes, which are easily feigned by any inmate who recognizes the game he or she has to play.[17] One writer has summed it up by declaring that

> the crazy-quilt collection of states of human distress which we lump together and label Mental Illness remains about as intractable to our schemes for social mastery and remediation—to say nothing of elimination—as was the case in antiquity.[18]

Some assessments conclude that organizations for helping the inadequate, the poor, and the wayward yield results that are perverse. Ivan Illich argues

[14] Ronald W. Maris, "The Psychology of Suicide Prevention," *Social Problems* 17 (Summer 1969): 132–49.

[15] Kenneth M. Colby, "Psychological Treatment of Mental Disorder," *Encyclopedia of the Social Sciences* 10 (1968): 176. A 1976 study found no relationship between measures of patient adjustment while still hospitalized and their posthospital success or recidivism. Barry Willer and Paul Bigger, "Comparison of Rehospitalized and Nonhospitalized Psychiatric Patients on Community Adjustment," *Psychiatry* 39 (August 1976): 239–45.

[16] Eysenck, *Crime and Personality*, p. 142.

[17] James R. Greenley, "Alternative Views of the Psychiatrist's Role," *Social Problems* 20 (Fall 1972): 252–62.

[18] Merton J. Kahne, in a book review in *Psychiatry* 35 (November 1972): 392.

School prepares for the alienating institutionalization of life by teaching the need to be taught. Once this lesson is learned, people lose their incentive to grow in independence; they no longer find relatedness attractive, and close themselves off to the surprises which life offers.[19]

"The real function of schools," Zeigler and Peak declare, is "the *covert* mobilization of bias." [20] They further conclude, from studies of curricula, that the emphasis on indoctrination is just as great in the United States as in Tanzania or Russia and probably more effective because it is less explicit and operates more through the latent content of the school program.[21] But it is also conspicuous in the manifest content. Hess and Torney found a repetitive emphasis in the schools on the values of loyalty, authority, and law, and an underemphasis on citizens' rights.[22]

A study of rehabilitation programs in prisons makes a similar point: that they "stunt the human potential by training programs that, as with animals, condition their subjects to an unthinking conformity to inflexible, externally imposed rules." The authors strike one optimistic note, stemming from the very ineffectiveness of this regimen: "In studying the criminal justice system we have found few things to be thankful for, but the ineffectiveness of correctional treatment may well be one of them." [23]

One of the more striking cases appears in a comparative study of two high schools. In one of these, misbehaving students were handled by classroom teachers, who were likely to define them in such terms as lazy, overly energetic, or in need of a kick in the

[19] Ivan Illich, *Deschooling Society* (New York: Harper and Row, 1971), p. 47.

[20] Harmon Zeigler and Wayne Peak, "The Political Functions of the Educational System," *Sociology of Education* 43 (Spring 1970): 122.

[21] Ibid., p. 121. See also Jonathan Kozol, *The Night Is Dark and I Am Far from Home* (Boston: Houghton Mifflin, 1976).

[22] Robert D. Hess and Judith Torney, *The Development of Political Attitudes in Children* (Chicago: Aldine, 1967), pp. 120–28. See also Edgar Litt, "Civic Education, Community Norms, and Political Indoctrination," *American Sociological Review* 28 (February 1963): 69–75; John C. Pock, U.S. Department of Health, Education, and Welfare, *Attitudes toward Civil Liberties among High School Seniors*, Cooperative Research Project No. 5–8167 (Washington, D.C.: Government Printing Office, 1967); Byron G. Massalias, "American Government: We Are the Greatest!" in C. Benjamin Cox and Byron G. Massalias, *Social Studies in the United States* (New York: Harcourt, Brace, and World, 1967).

[23] American Friends Service Committee, *Struggle for Justice*, p. 45.

pants. In the other school, which was larger and more bureaucratized, "problem" students were sent to counselors, social workers,
or psychologists, who were likely to apply a Freudian or other technical label to them ("obsessive–compulsive," "aggressive," "hostile")
and to require them to undergo continuing "treatment." The result
was significantly more problems stemming from the labeling and the
resulting pressure on the students to play their ascribed sick roles,
to rationalize their misconduct, and to justify the professional diagnosis and prescription.[24] One social worker referred to a student's
old and worn shoes as evidence he was trying to win the attention
of the school authorities. When the same student was tardy or
absent, she diagnosed it as an Oedipal conflict: "a means of avoiding
success and thus a means of being compared with other men in the
mother's life."[25]

Erving Goffman similarly observed labeling that became a self-fulfilling prophecy in a mental hospital,[26] and Jacobson and Rosenthal
observed it in a primary school.[27] Welfare recipients similarly feel
pressure to "play out the pathology attributed to them by their
social workers."[28]

[24] Aaron Cicourel and John I. Kitsuse, *Educational Decision-Makers* (Indianapolis, Bobbs-Merrill, 1963), p. 100.

[25] Ibid., pp. 112–13. For further evidence that ghetto schools confuse signs of
social class with signs of ability and then make their categories self-fulfilling
prophecies, see Roy C. Rist, "Student Social Class and Teacher Expectations: The
Self-Fulfilling Prophecy in Ghetto Education," *Harvard Educational Review* 40
(August 1970): 411–51.

[26] Erving Goffman, *Asylums* (New York: Doubleday Anchor, 1961).

[27] Robert Rosenthal and Lenore Jacobson, *Pygmalion in the Classroom:
Teacher Expectations and Pupils' Intellectual Development* (New York: Holt,
Rinehart, and Winston, 1968).

[28] Richard M. Elman, *The Poorhouse State: The American Way of Life on
Public Assistance* (New York: Wiley, 1964), pp. 291–92. Some other studies
pointing to the ineffectiveness or problematic effects of these kinds of organizations are: Colin Greer, *The Great School Legend* (New York: Basic Books, 1972);
Carl G. Carlson, Michael Hersen, and Richard M. Eisler, "Token Economy Programs in the Treatment of Hospitalized Adult Psychiatric Patients," *Mental
Health Digest* 4 (December 1972): 21–27; P. G. McGrath, "Custody and Release
of Dangerous Offenders," in *The Mental Abnormal Offender*, ed. A. deReuck
and R. Porter (Boston: Little, Brown, 1968); Henry J. Steadman, "The Psychiatrist
as a Conservative Agent of Social Control," *Social Problems* 20 (Fall 1972): 263–
71.

The effects of labeling and of societal reactions in shaping behavior remain
a problematic and controversial issue in social science. The following relatively

It can be argued that such studies miss the point: that they are arbitrary in setting benchmarks of success or that statistical averages are less important than the help even a few receive. But such objections make, rather than deny, the point that success, failure, and uncertainty hinge upon definitions and classifications. The consequences of administrative policies are readily redefined and as readily perceived in alternative ways. It is not facts that are crucial, but language forms and socially cued perceptions.

The objection also calls attention to a claim frequently voiced by critics of those organizations: that such successes as they do achieve come disproportionately from "creaming"—from devoting their resources largely to the people with the greatest chance of emerging as winners, with or without "help." [29] Put another way, creaming produces organizational effectiveness only in the sense that statistics show, not in the sense that the outcome would be very different if the organizations did not do whatever they do.

The Constriction of Administrative Staff

The common explanation for dubious administrative performance and for the frustrations clients suffer is staff inefficiency, incompetence, or stupidity. The staff may *be* inefficient or incompetent;

---

recent studies offer a range of perspectives: Walter R. Gove and Patrick Howell, "Individual Resources and Mental Hospitalization," *American Sociological Review* 39 (February 1974): 86–100; Thomas J. Scheff, "The Labelling Theory of Mental Illness," *American Sociological Review* 39 (June 1974): 444–52; Walter R. Gove, "The Labelling Theory of Mental Illness: A Reply to Scheff," *American Sociological Review* 40 (April 1975): 242–48; David Matza, *Becoming Deviant* (Englewood Cliffs, N.J.: Prentice-Hall, 1969); John I. Kitsuse, "Deviance, Deviants: Some Conceptual Problems," in *An Introduction to Deviance,* ed. William J. Filstead (Chicago: Markham, 1972); Prudence Rains, "Imputations of Deviance: A Retrospective Essay on the Labelling Perspective," *Social Problems* (October 1975): 1–11.

[29] A great many studies find pervasive creaming. As examples, see Gideon Sjoberg, Richard A. Brymer, and Buford Farris, "Bureaucracy and the Lower Class," in *The National Administrative System,* ed. Dean L. Yorwood (New York: Wiley, 1971), pp. 369–77; Frances F. Piven and Richard A. Cloward, *Regulating the Poor* (New York: Vintage, 1971), p. 176; John D. Owen, "Racial Bias in the Allocation of Teachers in Sixty-Nine Urban Elementary School Systems," Johns Hopkins University Center for the Study of Organization of Schools (Baltimore, November 1969); Cicourel and Kitsuse, *Educational Decision-Makers,* p. 140.

but it is often only in the sense that people are incompetent when they try to fly by flapping their arms. In a setting that is designed for constricted roles rather than for complete human beings, the complaint that individuals are ineffective is less a factual discovery than a political exhortation, a way of focusing popular attention on a symptom while diverting attention from the root problem: the systematic reasons for organizational ineffectiveness. The blaming of individuals leaves untouched the structure of roles that will continue to frustrate clients and staff members in the future. Heads roll readily at low levels of every organization. The challenge is to identify the specific characteristics of complex organizations that systematically generate both ineffective results and problematic beliefs and perceptions.

It is the clarity and rigidity with which roles are defined in formal organizations that distinguishes them from most informal social interactions. A staff member's raison d'être is to live up to particular role expectations, not to use all his or her faculties or knowledge to choose a course of action. Policemen are normally rewarded for their sensitivity to the value of "law and order," not for enlarging the civil liberties of alleged offenders or of the general public. The secretary of labor is not ordinarily expected to complain that workers' wage levels are too high, nor are other staff members in the Labor Department; but officials of the Treasury and Agriculture Departments *are* expected to do so. Predetermined action is legitimized by its presentation as the knowledgeable weighing of technical or professional considerations. Segmented people, sometimes as preprogrammed as machines, may still experience themselves as whole and self-acting, for the internalization of organizational objectives is not necessarily self-conscious.[30] In a special sense, then, the bureaucratic claim of impersonality is justified, for it is often roles, not whole persons, that function in complex organizations.

The critical psychological difference between an autonomous person and an occupant of a bureaucratic role lies in the grounds for his or her actions. The exercise of their faculties and talents exhilarates independent human beings. They paint or climb mountains or do craftsmanlike work or formulate ideas or designs because they can and because they feel fulfilled when they do. Insofar as a person is a

---

[30] See James G. March and Herbert A. Simon, *Organizations* (New York: Macmillan, 1958), chap. 3.

bureaucrat, he or she is motivated by the rewards and penalties built into the organization that confers the role: by anticipation of pay increases, discharge, praise or reprimands, promotions or demotions, desirable or undesirable job assignments, all at the discretion of superiors. Acts are motivated by positive or negative reinforcement; working life and much of nonworking life is Skinnerian. As in all successful behavior modification, the staff member learns to internalize the wants and values of his or her trainers, and in doing so becomes the constricted role he or she plays.

"Independent human being" and "bureaucrat" are analytic categories, of course, and are intermingled in everyday life and work. People and their jobs differ widely in how close they come to one or the other pole, and the difference can be critical.

The titles and job descriptions of bureaucratic positions call attention to skills and competences rather than to controls on an incumbent's performance; and so they help staff members to avoid recognizing the degree to which programmed rewards and punishments, rather than their own talents, shape their work and their lives. Here is a form of systematic reconstruction of facts through language that is central to quiescent acceptance of a bureaucratized society.

Bureaucratic roles serve the expectations of the agency's constituency: the group with power to cripple, scuttle, or change an agency that fails to meet its expectations.[31] Farm organizations exert strong influence at the top echelons of the Department of Agriculture and in the House and Senate Agriculture Committees, but the poor do not. Property owners and local industry, not ghetto residents, can influence personnel and budgetary decisions in a police department. The Office of Economic Opportunity had no politically potent constituency except that provided by occasional middle-class concern for the poor and by occasional militance from the Welfare Rights Organization. In each case, the unit adapts to the values and interests of its constituency. The agency attracts staff members who share its values, while those who do not either leave or remain in uninfluential positions.

The everyday work of the bureaucrat reinforces this internalization

[31] For a discussion of the functions of administrative constituencies, see Murray Edelman, "Governmental Organization and Public Policy," *Public Administration Review* 12 (Autumn 1952): 276–83.

of the values of his organizational unit's constituency. To the police-man patrolling a ghetto, every mugging becomes clearer evidence that the mugger is an evil who should be destroyed and that crim-inologists and liberals who see the mugger as a tragic product of his environment are either dupes or collaborators with evil. To a poverty lawyer the enforcement of the man-in-the-house rule is re-pression of the poor, not protection for the taxpayer. To an Agricul-ture Department undersecretary, grain is a source of income for the farmer rather than a means of helping the undernourished to survive.

An employee of the Bureau of Indian Affairs does not win promo-tions by reflecting the values or perceptions of the American Indian Movement (AIM) in his or her reports, and the access, flow, and categorization of information within the Bureau makes it easy for staff members to perceive AIM as misguided and without mass support.

In April 1972, the director of the Food Research and Action Cen-ter, a federally funded research agency, told the Senate Nutrition Committee that a survey showed that the Agriculture Department "knowingly misled" Congress by drastically underreporting the num-ber of schools that wanted breakfast programs for needy children. At least 4,900 schools had asked for the breakfasts, but the Agricul-ture Department reported there were only 1,100. The assistant secre-tary of agriculture responsible for the program acknowledged that these figures "would not be that far from being accurate," but still called the criticism "immature, unfair and intemperate." [32] For both the Department staff and its critics, values and ideology help shape beliefs about what is fact, which facts are relevant, and who is intemperate.

Daily enactment of a role that pits administrators' perceptions against counterperceptions requires either that they accept the values dominant in the organization or that they abandon the role and the job. The offender, the welfare rule, and the surplus commodity be-come symbols. Terms and organizational roles define each other and constrict the cognitive range of the role player.

Yet he or she remains a human being. With greater or lesser self-consciousness, and especially when he is playing roles outside the confines of his job, he feels some ambivalence, and somehow he ex-presses it: perhaps through more zealous acting out of his organi-

[32] *New York Times*, 11 April 1972, p. 21.

zational role to repress his doubts; perhaps through dedication in other activities to some of the values his work requires him to neglect; perhaps by assuming that other functionaries take care of the problem he neglects; perhaps through irony in the language in which he discusses his organizational ties. Everyone encounters examples of these modes of expressing ambivalence toward an organization. The first, resolution of doubt through zealous conformity to the role, is especially common. As members of organizations we are all somewhat constricted; but as human beings we must somehow reflect our potentialities for a more rounded cognitive range.

Because they suppress qualms, these modes of expression leave the bureaucrat more free to play his or her expected role without inhibitions; and because they rationalize bias in the selection and reconstruction of facts, they ensure that, in their most controversial activities, complex organizations will fairly often reach incorrect conclusions: incorrect even from the standpoint of achieving their own values.

Some staff members do not adapt to their expected roles, and the organization deals systematically with them as well. If they display their reservations in their work or their demeanor toward superiors, they may be discharged. More often, the role conflict they experience drives them to look for other work. The pattern is common in every organization that has a controversial objective and in every organization whose achievements are at odds with its ostensible purpose. Many social workers leave their jobs in a public agency after they find that they are spending most of their time on paperwork and in denying requests for help rather than in helping the needy. Some teachers' dreams of imparting exciting knowledge to the young become nightmares of imposing discipline and acting as a jailer or custodian, and many of them also leave.

But the displacement of staff who refuse to play a constricted role itself has a systematic consequence. It leaves the organization staffed with people who adapt, so that the prevailing definitions, ideology, and policy directions are constantly reinforced but seldom questioned.

The requirements of some roles are clearly enough understood that only those who are willing or eager to adapt to them accept them in the first place: the prison guard, the policeman, and often the probation officer, for example. In such cases, self-selection assures that staff members will carry out their expected functions without undue qualms. Constriction of perspective is the result, no matter which mechanism produces it. In advanced cases, everything is defined in terms of the organizational role. To the uptight policeman everyone is a potential offender. Schoolmarms of both sexes behave like teachers in the living room and when reacting to novels or to public affairs; they define their worlds according to the specialized perspective they have internalized. As one analyst has put it, "problem equals need, and need, in turn, equals the service they happen to have handy in the upper right hand drawer." [33] The constriction is rarely total, and in some organizations, such as those devoted to basic research, it may be minimal. The degree of its presence defines the degree to which an organization is bureaucratic.

Jurisdiction as a Deterrent to Effectiveness

A related reason for organizational ineffectiveness stems from incongruities between the goals of organizations and their legal powers. A welfare agency has no authority to provide what many of its clients chiefly need to get them off the welfare rolls: more jobs and better-paying ones. No matter how dedicated its staff may be to helping their clients, they are powerless to act in this key respect, though welfare organizations bear the major *symbolic* responsibility for coping with poverty. Other organizations—with different objectives and responsive to different constituencies—are *able* to influence employment and pay levels: chiefly the Treasury Department, the Federal Reserve Board, the Defense Department, the Commerce Department, and the Banking and Appropriations Committees of Congress. In none of these agencies are the poor even a nominal constituency, and all of them must be responsive to the interests of the business and banking communities in order to survive politically. A substantial amount of unemployment and inflation are often advantages, not evils, for these constituencies. While the establishment of agencies to serve each major economic interest symbolizes equity, actual allocations of jurisdiction and legal power produce advantages for those who have economic resources at their disposal. The Labor Department has little more influence over employment or pay levels than the Department of Health, Education, and Welfare or a county

---

[33] William Ryan, *Blaming the Victim* (New York: Pantheon, 1971), p. 246.

welfare department. The names for jurisdictional allocations constitute one of the most potent devices for divorcing organizational accomplishments from their symbolic evocations.

The Multiple Veto and Organizational Conservatism

When policy proposals, dockets, or case files in an agency require the comments and approval of a number of staff members to whom they are circulated, each official is likely to have special reasons for discouraging innovation or risk-taking. This is not true in the relatively rare situation that is regarded as either a dire emergency or as an occasion in which risk-taking will be widely supported: a severe depression, an enemy attack, or a crash program to send people to the moon. Such situations give rise to new organizations with an ethos that rewards risk-taking. But in ongoing agencies with fixed constituencies and fixed opposition, a strategy that minimizes risk-taking becomes part of the long-term staff member's mode of operation. He or she survives and advances so long as he does not disturb others and does not offend the organization's supporting constituency.

Circulating inside such an agency there is often an heroic tale of an official, often a founder of the organization, who once accomplished wonders through dramatic innovation; but the legend serves the function of revolutionary legends generally; it legitimizes the existing polity and its policies. In current operations, failures are hazardous so risks are minimized. Established courses of action assure, moreover, that failures will be blurred, delayed, attributed to different causes, or otherwise masked. That a sizable fraction of the population remains poor is not typically perceived as a failure of governmental fiscal policy, monetary policy, welfare policy, or of the economic system; but the grant by a caseworker of special benefits that a court or legislative committee later decides were unauthorized brings budget cuts and individual sanctions. Staff members learn early in their careers that the error stemming from zeal in behalf of clients, not the error likely to produce organizational ineffectiveness, is risky. The "quality control" reports the Department of Health, Education, and Welfare requires from state welfare departments reveal "much larger errors in the direction of keeping eligible people off the rolls than in permitting ineligible people on the rolls." [34]

In a psychiatric hospital it is part of the role of each separate type of professional to be ready with a different reason for caution in discharging a patient: the social worker because his home environment may be unsuitable (especially if he is poor); the nurse because he may not have adapted well to ward rules and authority;[35] the psychiatrist because he may not have resolved his psychodynamic problems or is "escaping to health." Each such response is predictable if the patient displays norms or values different from those of the staff; and the response benefits the staff member by proving his or her status and competence. The performance is patterned and stylized, though staff members define it as the exercise of professional judgment. Its effect on organizational policy is manifestly conservative.

Many believe that conservatism is desirable in such cases to protect the inmate and society, to prevent dangerous people from misbehaving; and every publicized offense by a former inmate renews this belief. This kind of cognitive structuring exemplifies the selective perception of information to reinforce established beliefs, for the perspective masks some serious and certain costs while focusing on an improbable and problematic one. Headlines about a crime by a former mental patient reinforce the common fear that mental patients are dangerous. Statistics showing that the crime rate for former mental patients is substantially lower than for the general population [36] are not news and are easily ignored even when they are published. Nor is it news or reassuring reinforcement of established beliefs that a great many people are involuntarily confined and deprived of dignity to minimize the possibility that a released inmate might do something to bring criticism on the staff. Information that reinforces widely held beliefs is noticed, emphasized, and fanta-

[34] Piven and Cloward, *Regulating the Poor*, p. 157.

[35] For a study that reached this conclusion, see B. E. Stoffelmayr, "The Relationship between Nurses' Ratings of Patient Behavior and Observed Patient Behavior," *Social Psychology* 8 (February 1973): 37–40.

[36] Bruce J. Ennis, *Prisoners of Psychiatry* (New York: Harcourt, Brace, Jovanovich, 1972), p. 225. Ennis calls attention to a study showing that in New York the arrest rate over a five-year period for 5,000 former mental patients was less than one-twelfth the rate for the community at large. Other studies reach similar conclusions.

sized; information that challenges them is masked or readily forgotten, both by bureaucrats and in the conservative opinions they help create. The legitimation of established practice and the evocation of anxiety about untried possibilities constitute a substantial part of the discourse of administrators, ensuring that feedback in organizations is selective.

But this is an outsider's description, for the language of the administrative staff member often defines the pursuit of established policy as innovative. In periods of economic expansion and rising prices administrators may refer to the adoption of a tight money policy that restricts credit as an experiment, though it is the classic response to that situation. Behavioral psychologists and psychiatric staff speak of the introduction of compulsory behavior modification programs as innovative or experimental, though the powerful have controlled the powerless since the dawn of history by rewarding them for conformity to accepted norms and punishing them for independence, idiosyncrasy, and irreverence. When military officers respond to allegations of a foreign threat by calling for more armament and a tough stance, they unfailingly define their ritualistic reaction as boldness and strategic calculation. The categorization of recurring behavior as original and creative manifestly helps administrators to enact their roles resolutely.

For the organization, though not necessarily for the client, conservatism of this sort is a minimax strategy and sometimes better than that, for its very ineffectiveness may intensify the need for the organization. A welfare system that eliminated poverty or a criminal justice system that minimized crime would work itself out of business; but the perpetuation of poverty and crime create broader support for the agencies that deal with them. The logic of such a system requires that the administrator's first loyalty be to the organization, not the client, in what he does even if not in the accepted rationale for it. The rule that works inequitably or ineffectively for a particular group of welfare recipients, defendants in the courts, or students is sacrosanct because it protects the organization against political sanctions. Even the client's attorney in a criminal trial serves the criminal justice system as a first priority. As an officer of the court and a member of the organized bar he or she assumes an organizational role; deviation from it in his client's interest brings severe economic and psychological sanctions or imprisonment for contempt

of court, as attorneys defending people charged with political offenses
have often learned.[37]

"Groupthink"

Administrators chronically subjected to criticism erect defenses.
Any group of officials who feel beleaguered by critics, whether justi-
fiably or not, are likely to develop a high degree of group loyalty,
to define outsiders who criticize them as ignorant of the problem,
confused, immoral, or not to be taken seriously for other reasons,
and to define supporters as the important segment of public opinion.[38]

Asking himself why so many fiascos should occur in foreign policy
in spite of the high intelligence and integrity of the people who
achieve influential posts in the State Department, the psychologist
Irving Janis sees the answer in "groupthink," which he defines as
"a deterioration of mental efficiency, reality testing, and moral judgment that results from in-group pressures." Loyalty to the group
comes to be considered "the highest form of morality." Its members
are not inclined to raise ethical issues that imply that " 'this fine
group of ours, with its humanitarianism and its high-minded princi-
ples, might be capable of adopting a course of action that is in-
humane and immoral.' " [39]

Janis's analysis is perceptive, though he may not adequately specify
the sense in which the in-group pressures within an organization
that develops these symptoms reflect outside pressures from its
constituency. Not only public criticism of their work but low public
esteem and low salaries create a strong emphasis on in-group loyalty,
accounting for its prevalence among low status members of all the
helping professions and especially among policemen, who suffer
both from criticism and from low pay.

[37] Abraham S. Blumberg, *Criminal Justice* (Chicago: Quadrangle, 1967).

[38] For a careful study showing that State Department officials selectively perceived public opinion in this fashion in the 1960s, see Bernard C. Cohen, *The
Public's Impact on Foreign Policy* (Boston: Little, Brown, 1973).

[39] Irving L. Janis, *Victims of Groupthink* (Boston: Houghton Mifflin, 1972),
p. 11.

Selective Feedback

Michael Crozier sees the absence of corrective feedback as the central characteristic of bureaucracy.[40] Analysis of bureaucratic language calls attention to the consistent highlighting of some kinds of information and the systematic neglect of other kinds, so that it may be more valid to speak of selective feedback; but Crozier is certainly right to see adequacy in feedback as crucial. The obvious deficiencies in feedback come about through failure to provide systematic means of learning about the unintended consequences of administrative actions. The more subtle and more serious deficiencies in feedback occur through the routine use of terms that characterize actions, clients, and results in such a way that failures will either be unrecognized or defined as inevitable.

The prevailing system of categorization excuses ineffective "rehabilitation" by defining anyone who fails to respond by such terms as "hard core," "chronic," "mentally deficient," "underachiever," and "sociopath." Ritualistic categorization further confuses feedback by defining a substantial proportion of the population as either pathological or prepathological, thereby ensuring that a large number so labeled will function more or less normally and so be seen as "successes." Not much must change in anybody except the terms that define them. The substitution of ideological naming for observation of the immediate and the unintended outcomes of organizational actions ensures that failures will normally be excused as inevitable or remain unrecognized, both inside and outside the organization.

The distortion of feedback processes leaves administrative staff more free to carry out the logic of their definitions of the situation. When poverty means cultural deprivation and cognitive deficiency to the slum teacher, "the primary effect of poverty, race, and family background is," as Ryan observes, "not on the children, but on the teacher, who is led to expect poorer performance from black and poor children." [41] Where rules have serious consequences for the rule-makers as well as those expected to comply with them, serious assessment of their impact is likely to be avoided in favor of "knowl-

[40] Michael Crozier, *The Bureaucratic Phenomenon* (Chicago: University of Chicago Press, 1964), chap. 8.
[41] Ryan, *Blaming the Victim*, p. 48.

edge" based on categorization. As Garfinkel puts it, "the more important the rule, the greater is the likelihood that knowledge is based on avoided tests." [42]

Distortion of feedback through categorization is common in all bureaucracies. The $85-a-week wages of the woman who mops the floors in a great corporation's office building is "income," taxed at the statutory rate, and the million-dollar increase in the building's market value is "capital gain," taxed at half the rate for income. Many other definitions in the tax code similarly justify benefits for the wealthy. In 1974, the cleaning women who worked for Exxon paid a higher proportion of their incomes in federal taxes than did the corporation, whose first quarter profits increased 38 percent that year,[43] exemplifying the effect of a tax labeled "progressive" and generally based on "ability to pay." Tax lawyers and IRS auditors do not try to produce perverse results. They carry out their duties in accordance with the legal categorizations, which protect them from confronting the perverse results, just as the cleaning women, the stockholders, and the general public are similarly protected and constricted.

Language that emphasizes the subordinate position of the people who do the work further deflects criticism of their decisions. Superiors make policy, while subordinates only carry it out; they are not exercising discretion or being arbitrary, but applying the rules, which they do not make. This assertion, which is the rhetorical hallmark of the bureaucrat, accomplishes several functions. It protects those who make the critical decisions from public criticism; it exalts superiors even when they are involved only rhetorically with the work for which they are credited; it degrades the status and the self-concept of subordinates even when they are making the critical decisions; and it helps persuade the interested public that people with specialized or professional training are making policy, even when they are not. The dramaturgy and the rhetoric of subordination to experts ordinarily suffices to maintain adequate public support for organizations, regardless of the specific impacts of their acts, because feedback is inadequate and the ultimate consequences of actions remote.

[42] Harold Garfinkel, *Studies in Ethnomethodology* (Englewood Cliffs, N.J.: Prentice-Hall, 1967), p. 70.

[43] *The Economist*, 6 April 1974, p. 48.

Paradoxically, the processing of decisions through a hierarchical chain often enhances the power of the subordinate to make key categorizations and key policy decisions, making feedback even more problematic. The staff member who initially makes a decision weighs a wide range of facts, but he does not report all of them in justifying his decision to his superiors in the organization. If he did, he would be unnecessary, for his superior would then be faced with just as complicated a decision.

Instead, the subordinate resolves uncertainties in order to reach conclusions in doubtful cases. Despite a high IQ, a student's mixed grades and insolent deportment suggest he should not be recommended to a good college. The welfare recipient's uncooperative attitudes suggest that a temporary cutoff of aid in spite of her poverty would benefit her by making her a more dependable person. Such conclusions become the premises on which superiors make their decisions about more general policy, while the uncertainties that faced the initial decision maker grow dim or are ignored in the interests of time and efficiency. The subordinate's conclusions become the superior's "facts." March and Simon recognize that "uncertainty absorption" of this kind is an inevitable influence upon organizational policy and that it can make superiors dependent on the judgments of their subordinates.[44] Superiors do sometimes overrule subordinates, especially when proposed actions might bring political or other sanctions. But subordinates cannot be overruled very often, for they then become a hindrance to the organization and either leave or are dismissed. The longer the hierarchical chain, the more likely that the subordinate's uncertainties will be absorbed and his or her conclusions shape decisions.

In such cases the language justifying the decision does call attention to pertinent facts, often including information suggesting a different decision from the one that is taken; but the categories in which the facts are placed rationalize the decision that has been reached. The student may have "latent" ability, but is a confirmed "underachiever." Both in the internal dossiers that influence superiors and in the formal opinion that justifies the organization's action to outsiders, uncertainties are resolved into more confident grounds for action.

[44] March and Simon, *Organizations*, chap. 6.

Bureaucratic Language as Incantation

A related characteristic of many official statements helps further to neutralize or win over potential opponents: the resort to jargon and banality. Bureaucratic language is usually dismissed as funny and trivial. But in politics, as in religion, whatever is predictable, ceremonial, or banal serves a function. The jargon of administrators does have important consequences, for its users and for public opinion, though the dictionary definitions of the words rarely convey their meaning.

Resort to jargon in any organization can be understood as an implicit expression of loyalty to the values that are dominant in that organization. The social worker who sees a "predelinquent'" where others see a destitute child, like any staff member who accepts stylized terms as natural, is proclaiming that just as his or her words are banal, so will his ideas be those that are expected of staff in that particular organization. He will not rock the boat or think innovatively.[45] He is an insider.

Bureaucratic banality takes another form as well. There are classic justifications of governmental policies that recur in response to criticism or fear of criticism, regardless of the agency, individuals, or subject matter involved. Like responsive readings in church, they dull the critical faculties of those who use them and those who hear them [46] and at the same time give developments a reassuring meaning, thereby mollifying the fears everyone holds of arbitrary or malevolent administrative action.

Obviously, administrators sometimes offer nonritualistic, adequate explanations of policies as well, but I focus here on those justifications that are banal in the sense that they are offered repeatedly in terms general enough to justify any policy.

The rationalizations recur because the kinds of anxieties official actions evoke recur. The most general of these is fear that a policy entails dangerous consequences for the people affected by it: the dispatch of troops to the borders of a hostile country; notice to

[45] For a more extended discussion of this form of administrative language, see Murray Edelman, *Politics as Symbolic Action* (New York: Academic Press, 1971), pp. 72–76.

[46] George Orwell makes the point in his brilliant essay "Politics and the English Language," in *A Collection of Essays* (Garden City, N.Y.: Doubleday, 1957).

parents that their child has an appointment with the school social worker or psychiatrist; an announcement to welfare recipients that their eligibility is being reassessed. The stock official response to public anxieties is the declaration that the action that arouses them is "routine," implying that it is not a calculated response to a specific current problem. If public fears of that action nonetheless turn out to be well founded, the responsible staff member can be expected to tell those who complain that he or she is only following policies laid down by law or by superiors: "I don't make the rules." "I am only doing my job." These classic forms of rebuff to clients are clearly a signal that the bureaucrat in question feels some qualms, if only subconsciously, and it usually means as well that he or she in fact had some discretion about the course of action. More generally, any resort to ritualistic rationalizations signals an administrator's recognition that he or she may be acting unfairly or ineffectively and that public reassurance is appropriate.

Still other recurring responses justify actions that hurt or punish people who have not committed an offense generally regarded as justifying punishment: the eviction of residents from a neighborhood designated for an expressway or for urban renewal, for example, or the involuntary incarceration or drugging of people whose behavior is unconventional or "emotionally disturbed." The common justification of such measures claims that the action is a form of therapy or rehabilitation that will leave the client better off than he was: a prediction that sometimes is valid and often is not; but because the consequences are rarely clear and knowledge of them rarely available, it is the assertion, not the results, that matters in shaping the beliefs of people who are not hurt themselves. A similar rationalization, especially common among policemen and psychiatric staff, declares that people really want to be disciplined and controlled even if they complain about it, for they value authority and fear uncontrolled independence. This form of rhetoric becomes especially frequent in authoritarian states and institutions.

Sometimes the bureaucratic justification recognizes that people are being hurt but sees that result as helpful, because deprivation encourages self-reliance. The welfare mother will learn to cope better, for example, if she cannot rely on food stamps or a monthly check, and it will induce her to accept counseling and less money. The New York City welfare manual declares that because dependency is unwholesome and should be discouraged, it is often as important to withhold assistance as to give assistance [47]—an instance of a banality rationalizing a non sequitur. This doctrine makes the staff and the general public feel better about refusals to grant assistance. Whether it makes the claimant self-reliant is more doubtful, for it certainly imposes strong pressure on the applicant to accept a counselor's view of how he or she should live. The same form of response serves every government agency with power to withhold benefits or to impose sanctions. It may sometimes be a valid position, of course, but it serves its political and psychological purpose, whatever its effects in a particular case—which few who use it or hear it ever can know.

A stronger form of the same claim recurs whenever the harm done is very great and very clear. In such instances the classic response holds that it is necessary to destroy in order to save. The American captain who announced in 1968 that he had to destroy a Vietnamese village in order to save it was echoing a litany incanted in thousands of tragic situations through the ages: revolutionaries who justify executions on the ground that, "You can't make an omelet without breaking some eggs"; the Spanish Inquisition that burned heretics in order to save their souls; psychiatrists who justify psychosurgery and sensory deprivation on the grounds that they have to destroy a sick personality to create a wholesome one; Nazis who defined the extermination of Jews as a "final solution." It appears that people can deliberately hurt others only by persuading themselves and as wide a public as possible that it serves a therapeutic purpose. The harm done is immediate and concrete while the salvation is remote, problematic, and perhaps nonexistent, or so it seems to the outsider. To people who accept the authorities' categorization of the situation, the rosy future dominates the scene, the official becomes the savior through his or her exercise of discretion, while the measures he uses are only means to an end and trivial by comparison. Alternative categorizations create multiple realities.

Another set of stock responses issues from organizations that fear criticism of their ineffectiveness. The most common form of rationalization is exaggeration of the record. Whatever has been done or planned becomes "historic," "original," or "innovative." An underfinanced and uncoordinated reaction to widespread destitution becomes a "war on poverty," when it is hardly a border skirmish in

[47] Piven and Cloward, *Regulating the Poor*, p. 156.

the eyes of the poor or of social scientists who study its impact.[48] A 1966 amendment to the Social Security Act specifying that agencies might require welfare recipients to accept counseling services as a condition for receiving cash payments was hailed as "a major landmark" in welfare history, though the approach would soon prove harmful and be officially abandoned within five years. Supplementing grandiose claims in such situations are heroic tales of an agency's successes in particular cases, almost always without evidence that the cases are typical or that the successes were lasting.

Clearly, administrative rationalizations take recurring forms that serve to "sharpen up the pointless and blunt the too sharply pointed," in Kenneth Burke's phrase. More specifically, they evoke an attractive future or a dark past that justifies the uses public officials make of their discretion. While highlighting the remote, the immediate impact of a measure is presented in ambiguous and dim terms.

Such rhetoric helps marshal support for policies, but it is the organization's place in a structure of interests, sanctions, and roles that shapes the policies in the first place. Administrators and a supportive outside public are tempted to confuse the functions of rhetoric with the functions of interests, sanctions, and ideologies, for the confusion helps all concerned to reconcile their qualms, their hopes, and their material interests into a pattern of support or of acquiescence.

Naturally enough, the assent of the people whose lives are directly affected by problematic measures is most effective in stilling the anxieties of officials and of the interested public. Banal bureaucratic rationalizations make it likely that an inattentive public will echo the authorities' responses, converting a policy that was dubious or that failed into a rhetorical success. Clients who are susceptible to organizational sanctions must display support more explicitly, especially for policies that look punitive to the naive observer. The prisoner, the mental patient, and the misbehaving student must show "insight" into their waywardness and their need for conventional norms before they can be allowed to live their lives autonomously. The citizen who has fallen into political heresy is forgiven

[48] See, for example, Sidney Lens, "Shriver's Limited War: How Much Has It Altered the Social Structure?" in *The New Politics of American Policy*, ed. Edgar Litt (New York: Holt, Rinehart, and Winston, 1969), pp. 376–80.

and rewarded when he or she confesses and recants. If the beneficiaries say "Amen" at the conclusion of services, the audience
shares the reassurance.

Conclusion

Public administrative organizations shape *beliefs* about their work
and their impact on society rather more effectively than they cope
with poverty, ignorance, crime, and emotional disturbance.

The structuring of cognitions inside a governmental organization
and the structuring of "outside" opinion about its activities reflect
each other through evocative language and actions with systematic
consequences. The very terms that purport to describe clients, policies, and impacts evoke public beliefs and perceptions, as do asser-
tions about "public opinion." The process works subtly, for the
most part through the establishment of bureaucratic role structures
responsive to groups that wield political sanctions and through
selective feedback that defines problematic effectiveness as success.

The Language of Inquiry
and the Language of Authority

Skeptical search for truth is bound before long to collide with established norms and authority. Tension between the pursuit of knowledge and social solidarity is an inherent characteristic of politics and of political man.

This chapter explores the subtle ways in which some terms, syntactic structures, and grammatical orders help create a posture of political loyalty while others facilitate free inquiry, skepticism, and experimentation. Both kinds of language recur constantly in public discussions and governmental proceedings, usually intermixed with each other. Regardless of the dictionary meanings of the words, the forms serve as symbols that encourage loyalty or skepticism. Their combination in actual usage often helps bolster authority by evoking the belief that science sanctions status distinctions, social norms, and role structures.

Basil Bernstein once used the terms "formal language" and "public language" to distinguish language forms that deal with explicit distinctions and qualifications from those that encourage sensitivity to a particular pattern of social interaction.[1] His dichotomy seems appropriate for analyzing a number of *political* language forms that convey meanings not always apparent in their manifest structures. I distinguish common political language constructions associated with a posture of skeptical inquiry from others that evoke a posture of loyalty, whether to governmental authorities or to other organizations, including political oppositions. This analysis needs to be read with the caveat in mind that the distinction between the two basic language styles is an *analytic,* not an empirical one, for they are combined in practice. The latter part of the chapter explores the effects on political beliefs and perceptions of the empirical combination of the two language forms in actual usage.

Formal Language

Formal language explicitly calls the attention of user and audience to the separate elements of propositions: factual allegations and their contingencies, logical relationships and their modifications and stress, individual qualifications, temporal and spatial relationships, the expression of affect, and the possibilities of alternative conceptualizations to organize experience. A self-conscious focus upon these elements entails two mental processes that the employment of a public language discourages: (1) continuous reexamination of the validity of both factual and logical propositions and a search for more adequate propositions; (2) efforts to explore the innovative possibilities of recombinations of facts, premises, inferences, and associated affect; that is, experimentation with cognitive structures. Twentieth-century concern with the irrational and nonrational may tempt us to underestimate the part that self-conscious skepticism and the deliberate search for information, whether dissonant or not, play in the formulation of beliefs and perceptions.

Mathematical propositions are manifestly close to a pure case of a formal language. Attention is focused upon logical relationships. This is so because numbers are abstractions from the content of propositions, abstractions that leave behind virtually all of the content that might identify the observer with particular beliefs and

[1] Basil Bernstein, *Class, Codes, and Control: Theoretical Studies Towards a Sociology of Language* (New York: Schocken Books, 1975), pp. 42–59.

perceptions. Abstraction would seem to be a critical characteristic of a formal language.[2]

A less obvious characteristic of mathematical language is also crucial and helps us identify other modes of formal language that play a part in the political process. In pursuing his calculations, the mathematician is self-consciously testing the possibilities of his or her mind—aware that the cognitive structures he builds are his own doing, not objective fact.[3] This form of awareness, inherent in formal languages, is absent and even regarded as contaminating in public languages, as we shall see shortly.

If these are the characteristics and the functions of formal language, what nonmathematical forms does it take in politics? First, in the degree that terms designate and analyze political processes—as distinguished from the characteristics of persons, problems, or institutions—they are manifestly abstractions and, like numbers, amount to challenges to play with their possibilities through recombinations of elements and a focus upon logical relationships and qualifications. Bernstein speculates that the percentage of nouns to verbs may be higher in a public language than in a formal language and suggests that, if this is true, the former "tends to emphasize *things*, rather than *processes*."[4]

Political examples of a focus upon processes are common: exploration of the alternative implications of organizing an agency by subject matter area, by professional skill, or by function; analysis of the comparative utilities of indirect or direct regulation of prices and wages; calculation of the optimal degree of centralization of a governmental function. Each such analysis is typically less formal, because less abstract, than a wholly mathematical calculation; but the degree of abstraction is sufficient that the analysis *can* be largely formal and somewhat independent of the "things" to which it will eventually be applied. Cognitive structures are built upon such terms as: "price increment," "jurisdiction by function," and "span of control." That analyses of such processes respecting one policy area are often used as models to suggest their likely consequences in a different area is evidence of a significant degree of formality and

[2] For a supportive and intriguing set of hypotheses on this theme, see Suzanne K. Langer, *Philosophical Sketches* (London: Oxford University Press, 1962).

[3] Jean Piaget, *Structuralism* (New York: Basic Books, 1971), pp. 17–36.

[4] Bernstein, *Class, Codes, and Control*, p. 44.

abstraction. The organization of agencies by function, substantive issue, or clientele, and the implications of different degrees of centralization are examples.

There is a third kind of formal political language, less commonly employed in an explicit way in public policy analysis but widely used nonetheless both by citizens and by public officials. It rests on self-conscious efforts to see situations from the perspective of other people whose everyday lives are part of those situations. Ethnomethodologists try to do this systematically, and more formally; but everyone has to try to perceive from others' perspectives in order to guide his own actions. The police chief who asks himself how a tense crowd will react if he uses force to halt a protest; the welfare administrator who asks himself whether liberalizing a benefit will satisfy a Welfare Rights Organization and whether it will bring punitive legislation from conservatives in the legislature; workers who ask themselves whether a strike will win them popular sympathy or an antiunion backlash—all of these people are trying to probe the phenomenological worlds of others and making calculations based on terms that represent abstractions from those worlds. Words commonly employed in this way include "tension," "mediation," "diversion," "schism," "anger," "ambiguity," "ambivalence," "appeal."

These are especially revealing forms of political inquiry; for it is by identifying with others, not by objectifying them and separating them from himself or herself, that the observer finds the provisional facts, concepts, and logical links with which he can play and make his calculations. Self-conscious recognition that the play of the observer's mind gives meaning to what he observes frees him or her to think imaginatively and abstractly, recombining elements into new cognitive structures and then testing their utility in interpreting events and behavior. The very mode of naming and thinking calls attention to its tentative character, its continuous need for testing or reformulation.

By contrast, terminologies and syntax that separate the observer and his premises from what he is studying tempt him into dogma; for such linguistic forms present what is observed as objective, as "fact" for any reliable observer (that is, any observer who employs the same language and method).

Art forms constitute still another formal language, one whose function in shaping political perceptions is seldom recognized because there is little general awareness of how art conveys information and meaning. Suzanne Langer's brilliant analyses of "presentational forms" are eye-opening in this regard, though their categorization as "aesthetic theory" has inhibited appreciation of their wider applications. Langer demonstrates that painting, sculpture, dance, poetry, and music convey information and meaning, but do so through relationships among their formal elements rather than through the sequential propositions of expository prose.[5] Art forms teach their audience to see new meanings in formal relationships in space and in time, and they provide understanding of emotion and of its relation to form (rather than directly expressing emotion). The artist and the audience can play with recombinations of elements and learn something about the potentialities for new patterns, that is, for building original cognitive structures. Plainly, all the characteristics of formal language are here: abstraction, the challenge of recombining forms regardless of their particular content, the self-conscious use of the mind to achieve new possibilities and new meaning.

Presentational forms also *inhibit* experimentation and the play of the mind, rather than freeing them, reinforcing conventional beliefs and acceptance of authority. This is surely their most common political function. When they do so, they constitute a public language, not a formal language. Yet art does sometimes serve as a formal political language, leading people to new insights and to perceptions of new possibilities. The best political cartoonists, like Honoré Daumier and David Levine, puncture conventions and excite their audiences to a search for different perceptions without resorting to expository prose. The best of the guerrilla theater of the sixties did the same thing, as good political satire has always done. Political oratory that excites the mind through unexpected evocations—the oratory of Cicero and some of the best of Lincoln, Bryan, and Franklin Roosevelt—can also be classified as art and as formal language in this sense, though it is of course intermingled with exposition and with public language.

The feeling in liberating political art forms is recognized as springing from the exhilaration of seeking and finding insights and playing with abstractions. Emotion is not confused with logic or perception.

[5] Suzanne K. Langer, *Philosophy in a New Key* (Cambridge, Mass.: Harvard University Press, 1946).

Just as a formal language is precise in its statements of fact and of logical relationships, and in distinguishing reasons from conclusions, so it is also explicit in distinguishing affect from meaningful propositions. Public language, by contrast, encourages its user and his audience to confuse reasons with conclusions and affect with meaning.

To the degree that people use one or another formal language, then, they find gratification in finding pertinent data and logical linkages in order to understand and act effectively. Cognitive dissonance and cross-pressures are part of the search and are sought out rather than avoided. The employment of formal language entails weighing conflicting perspectives, tentatively perceiving objectives and dangers from the vantage point of different social groups, and anticipating the outcomes of alternative strategies, for these processes are a part of free inquiry. To use formal language is to remain aware of the intimate link between how one thinks, what one perceives, and what conclusions are reached.

The following excerpt from the *Report of the National Advisory Commission on Civil Disorders* is an example of fairly formal language. I choose this particular illustration in order to contrast it later with an example of public language on the same subject:

> While Negro fertility rates, after rising rapidly to 1957, have declined sharply in the past decade, white fertility rates have dropped even more, leaving Negro rates much higher by comparison:

> Live Births per 1,000 Women
> Age 15–44

Year	White	Nonwhite	Ratio of Nonwhite to White
1940	77.1	102.4	1.33
1957	117.4	163.4	1.39
1965	91.4	133.9	1.46

> . . . the proportion of Negroes in the total population has risen from 10.0 percent in 1950 to 10.5 percent in 1960 and 11.1 percent in 1966. . . . If this trend continues, one of every eight Americans will be Negro by 1972.[6]

---

[6] *Report of the National Advisory Commission on Civil Disorders* (New York: Bantam Books, 1968), p. 238.

Whenever contemplated courses of action are expressed in terms that highlight their problematic or indeterminate character, relevant evidence is likely to be welcomed, whether or not it is consistent with other evidence and with tentative conclusions. Peter Sperlich has shown that many people seek out conflicting evidence in the course of deciding how to vote in elections.[7] Manifestly, public officials, professionals, and citizens do so with respect to where and when to build schools, locate welfare offices and post offices, plan mail delivery systems, and thousands of other choices.

Obviously, no person could long survive without some use of formal language, and neither could a polity; for problem solving and effective action would be wholly sacrificed to the demands of social unity and authority. But formal language always coexists with public language.

Public Language

People can communicate in a public language when they sufficiently share norms that they need not be explicit about premises and meanings. Simple and sometimes unfinished sentences, unconventional syntax, frequent repetition of a small number of idiomatic phrases, little qualification, and reliance on the very incompleteness of exposition to demonstrate implicit understanding between speaker and audience (Bernstein refers to "sympathetic circularity" [8]) all presuppose common norms that the language both reflects and reinforces. The language of Richard Nixon and his associates as heard on the White House tapes exemplifies the characteristics of a public language.

Rather than abstracting formal elements that can be reordered to yield new possibilities, public language validates established beliefs and strengthens the authority structure of the polity or organization in which it is used. It is therefore preeminently the language form supporters of regimes or organizations rely on to demonstrate to others and to themselves that they deserve support, to minimize guilt, to evoke feelings in support of the polity, and to engender suspicion of alternatives and of people identified as hostile. Bernstein

[7] Peter W. Sperlich, *Conflict and Harmony in Human Affairs: A Study of Cross-pressures and Political Behavior* (Chicago: Rand McNally, 1971).

[8] Bernstein, *Class, Codes, and Control*, p. 46.

suggests that it "tends to be . . . a 'tough' language," eliciting behavior consonant with the toughness and discouraging verbalization of tender feelings and the opportunities for learning inherent in the verbal expression of tender feelings.[9]

Public language takes many political forms. Exhortations to patriotism and to support for the leader and his or her regime are an obvious form. I focus here on the less obvious forms.

(1) *Terms classifying people (individually or in groups) according to the level of their merit, competence, pathology, or authority.* Deserving (or undeserving) poor, superior or subnormal IQ, skilled diplomatic negotiator, authoritarian personality, public-spirited businessman. All these purport to be descriptive terms, based on observations or reliable inference from observations. Yet each one of them takes for granted a great deal that is controversial, unknown, or false. That a poor person who is old or sick is deserving, while one who cannot find work or is paid wages below the subsistence level is not, is hardly self-evident. How much of what an IQ measures is class-based or culture-based? How much of the skill attributed to an official reflects approval of his values? Such terms classify people according to their alleged merits without calling attention to the complicated and controversial assumptions, inferences, omissions, likelihood of error, and alternative possibilities open to those who use the terms. Their use in political discussion discourages the tentativeness and continuing critical stance toward the mental processes of the observer that are the hallmark of science. Though such categorizations are closer to dogma than to science, they evoke elaborate cognitive structures in the public that takes the language forms to be precise and scientific. They justify status levels, but purport to be based on personal qualities: intelligence, skills, moral traits, or health.

One manifest lesson of this form of public language is that imprecision and the failure to distinguish among reasons, conclusions, and feeling can characterize language that is grammatical and that purports to be precise. The test does not lie only in whether statements are incomplete in form, but in whether they are incomplete in fact because of the failure to be explicit about what is taken for granted and therefore to keep conclusions tentative and distinct from

[9] Ibid., p. 48.

premises. For that reason Bernstein's focus upon speech forms, though suggestive, fails to go far enough in explicating the distinction between public and formal languages. Yet, there is a formal test for this form of public language; it lies in the unqualified employment of any term that specifies the level of merit of a person or group of people. Like all public language, its lexicon varies with the social milieu. The terms "wop," "nigger," and "dink" connote a level of merit while denoting an ethnic or national group. Qualifiers stating the premises of speakers are omitted because they point to what the speakers do not wish to face. The same is true of the usage of public language forms in more educated circles.

Casual references to terms of this sort help create popular biases regarding which people deserve support and which need to be controlled. Though such cognitions engender support for a great deal of legislation and adjudication, the subtlety and complexity of their generation and functioning leave them largely free of criticism, except among a comparatively small set of skeptics and scholars.

(2) *Terms that implicitly define an in-group whose interests conflict with those of other groups.* The White House tapes exemplify this common form of public language. The evocations of allies and enemies are implicit and indirect (when they are explicit, as in the formulation of military strategy and tactics, the language is formal, not public), occurring through such phrases as "stonewalling," "the hang-out road," references to the reliability, gullibility, or hostile stance of individuals, and the employment of terms like "loyalty," a word that also appeared more and more frequently in the Lyndon Johnson White House as opposition to Johnson escalated.

Terms of these kinds permeate the everyday language of pressure groups, political party activists, social movement activists, revolutionaries, business rivals, and organized crime, though the particular lexicon naturally varies with the historical period and the cultural milieu. By reinforcing social pressures for loyalty and support, and perceptions of a threat from outsiders, such terms continuously create and strengthen intergroup hostilities. Their employment by any group, together with the provocative behavior they encourage, also elicits their counteruse by the outsiders they define as adversaries. They create cognitions all the more effectively because, like all public language, they subtly evoke beliefs that are not made explicit and therefore are rarely questioned. Metaphor and metonymy spread the belief that academics or bankers are "enemies." The lack of explicit statement encourages the implicit but strongly felt view that electoral adversaries of Nixon are enemies of the state; to take that for granted as fact itself becomes public evidence of loyalty to the group.

It is one of the most significant political characterisitics of public languages that their employment in purer and purer form becomes a signal of in-group acceptance. Sentences become less and less complete and qualifiers more blatantly omitted as more and more is taken for granted, premises are more often left unquestioned, group ties grow stronger, and outside groups are perceived as more dangerous. As always, linguistic expression and psychological traits reflect and reinforce each other.

An excerpt from a speech delivered on July 30, 1966 in Detroit by Stokely Carmichael exemplifies this type of public language:

> I'm a little bit surprised that Lyndon Baines Johnson, the racist president of this country, can stand up and draw color lines and say ninety percent against ten percent—he said it, he drew the color lines. And all the good white folk in the country didn't say to him, "Hunh-uh Lyndon, it's not based on color." They all said, "Well, what you going to do? You only ten percent." Yeah, we ten percent, brother, but we strewed strategically all over your country, and we've got black brothers in Vietnam (shouts and applause). We have black brothers in your army and they may not have woken up yet, but, baby, if you mess with us inside in this country, you going to have a war in Vietnam (applause). You going to have a war in Vietnam (continued applause).[10]

(3) *Presentational forms that justify actions and policies.* Aesthetic and other presentational forms without a vocabulary can constitute a formal language, as suggested earlier; but when they are part of the governmental process, they more commonly serve as a public language, reinforcing conventional beliefs and acceptance of the social structure. Ceremonies, settings, and ritualistic procedures are conspicuous in every aspect of the governmental process, though we learn to see them as serving instrumental purposes. Election campaigns, legislative procedures, administrative hearings, judicial proceedings, summit meetings and other diplomatic interactions, and the public speeches and announcements of officials and of pressure group spokesmen are all heavily imbued with stylized and ritualistic

---

[10] Robert L. Scott and Wayne Brockriede, eds., *The Rhetoric of Black Power* (New York: Harper and Row, 1969), pp. 86–87.

components that justify policy to mass audiences. Policy formation is carried out largely in a language so intermingled with the stylized forms that participants and audiences typically attribute an instrumental function to the latter as well; yet it is impossible to grasp the full import of governmental procedures without making the analytical distinction. An economist's testimony at a legislative hearing on income maintenance plans is likely to be quite formal in content and may influence policy; but the setting in which he or she is heard is a presentational form evoking public confidence in the care and fairness of the proceedings. And this is often his only function; for the use of expert witnesses as a "cover" for deals already negotiated is a common legislative device.[11]

The symbolic import of routine governmental procedures is expression of the public will through balanced weighing of the needs of interested groups and rational choice based on expert counsel.[12] The public display that accompanies the routines evokes this reassuring meaning, while it minimizes the aspects of governmental policy-making about which there is general anxiety: bargaining among powerful groups at the expense of those who are not represented; the inadequacies or biases of experts and authorities; the possibility of error, injustice, deprivation, and inequality in benefits and in sacrifice.

The presentational forms that permeate the governmental process are not all equally good as art or equally effective in conveying their symbolic import. For a part of their audience, the committee hearings conducted by Senator Joseph McCarthy in the 1950s did not legitimize his actions, though for many they did so. By contrast, the felicitous phrases of Winston Churchill profoundly deepened the sense of community and the loyalty not only of Britons but of citizens of all the Allied powers in World War II.

The Empirical Combination of Formal and Public Languages

Political processes ordinarily are carried on through language that intermingles the formal and the public types. Some examples already

---

[11] Gilbert Y. Steiner and Samuel K. Gove, *Legislative Politics in Illinois* (Urbana: University of Illinois Press, 1961), chap. 4.

[12] I have analyzed these issues in some detail in Murray Edelman, *The Symbolic Uses of Politics* (Urbana: University of Illinois Press, 1964), chap. 7.

cited suggest that their combination in the same setting reinforces both; for the loyalty to a social structure encouraged by a public language draws support from its presentation as rational analysis, while the stimulation of inquiring into new possibilities is all the greater when it is associated with cherished group ties or patriotism.

It is tempting to pigeonhole individuals as intelligent or unintelligent according to the frequency and sophistication with which they use formal language. Because the two language forms are rarely separated in practice, this common form of categorization is still another instance of the problematic consignment of people to different levels of merit and competence, in turn justifying controls over them or their elevation to positions of influence and authority.

We learn to ascribe a high degree of formality and rationality to the utterances of educated people, especially if they express themselves in the conventional speech of the upper middle class, and to derogate the conventional speech of the working class and the poor as imprecise, sloppy, and impoverished. This classification scheme obviously reinforces disparities in political influence based on social class and educational level. Though Bernstein carefully explains that working-class speech patterns are not a consequence of a limited vocabulary and that a language code is independent of measured intelligence, he does take the position that the impoverished culture of working-class children induces a relatively low level of conceptualization. He concludes that working-class children use a language code that restricts learning and personal development, while sensitizing the child to his or her social structure and to the need for meeting its demands upon him. The middle-class child, by contrast, learns both a restricted and an "elaborated" language code, the latter enabling him or her to conceptualize more abstractly and develop in a more autonomous way.[13]

It is doubtful that Bernstein is justified in positing a systematic link between class level, on the one hand, and verbal deprivation and the ability to use formal language, on the other. William Labov's studies of the speech of black children in the urban ghettos seem to

[13] See Basil Bernstein, *Class, Codes, and Control: Volume I* (London: Routledge and Kegan Paul, 1971), chap. 9.

demonstrate that these children receive as much verbal stimulation, hear as many well-formed sentences, and participate as fully in a highly verbal culture as do middle-class children. Labov also finds that urban black children acquire the same basic vocabulary and the same capacity for conceptualization and for logic as anyone else who learns to speak and understand English. They do often speak a "nonstandard English," which can create problems for them in school and in applying for jobs, but it in no way inhibits the development of logical thought; for the logic of standard English is indistinguishable from the logic of any nonstandard English dialect by any test yet tried.[14]

I therefore believe that the analytic distinction between formal and public language is misused when individuals or classes of people are associated with either category. The distinction is useful in political language analysis because it enables us to probe: (1) the consequences for cognition of the intermingling of the two forms and (2) the political consequences of the problematic perception that some groups are inhibited in their capacity to reason and otherwise manipulate symbols while others are competent to do so. The second point has already been discussed; it provides a rationale for controlling people who are already in a deprived position in the social structure.

The first point is more complicated and more subtle, for the political impact of the intermingling of formal and public language can be discerned only by examining people's behavior in problematic situations in order to build hypotheses about the structure of their cognitions.

Consider some problematic situations. In tense times, urban guerrilla leaders typically make statements that shock the middle class: threats to employ terrorism (often accompanied by action) and to kill opposition leaders, and rhetoric exalting violence. Such language would seem to be close to the modal case of public language. It typically consists of short, incomplete sentences, confounds reasons and conclusions to produce categorical statements, repeats idiomatic phrases frequently, and relies upon "sympathetic circularity" among adherents of the movement to induce support for the social structure the guerrillas favor.

---

[14] William Labov, "The Logic of Nonstandard English," in *Language and Poverty*, ed. Frederick Williams (Chicago: Markham, 1970), pp. 153–89.

Yet those who use it often display strategic and tactical ability of a high order, recognizing and using the *strategic* potentialities of their public language. A major function of the blatant use of shocking rhetoric, for example, is to induce their adversaries to over-react and thereby alienate their own potential support. When there is sufficient tension and the language of the contending groups is appropriate, still greater tension and more serious confrontation follow. As this happens, the appeal of groups trying to bring about detente weakens, and the formal language component of the contending groups becomes less important. There is, then, a systematic link between the escalation of conflict and the possibility of wide support for flexible policies based on the abstraction and restructuring of formal elements in a problematic situation. With increasing confrontation, the role of public language grows more salient. As it does so, attachment to existing authority structures and to conventional definitions of the situation becomes more rigid.

To consider another example, economists and statisticians calculating the benefits and costs of alternative forms of a negative income tax plan employ formal language that is largely mathematical in its terms and syntax. But economists differ from their computers in the language mix they employ and in its psychological resonance: They can never keep their language on the purely formal plane. They may justify their calculations, for example, on the ground that a negative income tax scheme more effectively helps the poor than a plan that vests discretion in administrators to grant or withhold benefits, knowing as they do so that this is a controversial proposition relying in part on unstated premises and sympathies, and entailing a more influential role for economists and a less influential one for social workers than the opposite proposition. Their use of a formal language does not detract from either their ability or their incentive to use a public language as well. The two are typically intermingled, usually in unselfconscious and subtle modes of expression.

The second example (a negative income tax) carries with it a wider range of potential lines of political development than the first case (terrorist confrontation). It is less determinate in the courses of action and of language styles that may occur in the future. Opinions are less fixed and less emotional, there is play for a large number of possible conceptualizations and political compromises, and the economic conditions that form the background of the situation can change in many ways. These characteristics of the problematic situation obviously mean that the formal language component is more central than in the earlier example. *It is, then, the characteristics of the situation, not the abilities of the people involved in it, that determine the relative prominence of each language style.* This systematic tie is a central fact of politics.

Obviously, some individual differences do exist in the capacity to speak and think formally. They may stem from formal training, which provides particular skills. In tense political situations, people who prefer formal thinking may play a minor role and in calm situations they may play a major one; but individuals who do not shift easily between both forms are exceptional. Their very atypicality makes them conspicuous and evokes a categorization scheme that is too easily generalized.

Roles as Distinct from Human Beings

Though human beings rely on both forms of language and thought, the roles individuals play during their working day may not. Common political situations and organizational settings permit officials, administrators, economists, clinical psychologists, social workers, and other "policymakers" to remain in their positions of authority only so long as they hold to the norms that are taken for granted within the organization that employs them. When the White House, the congressional agriculture committees, and the secretary of agriculture accord higher priority to farmers' economic interests than to those of welfare beneficiaries in administering the surplus commodities program, an assistant secretary of agriculture with jurisdiction over that program is appointed to his post because he accepts that priority and will predictably resign or be dismissed if his actions reflect the opposite priority. The same is true of lower-level administrative staff members; though, if they are low enough, the penalty may be limited to reversal of their actions and possibly denial of promotions. Free inquiry may be severely inhibited by organizational sanctions that are occasionally explicit but typically function subtly through self-selection, selective recruitment and promotion, and through the pervasive use in an organization of a bureaucratic jargon that evokes "sympathetic circularity" for established norms and values. That is the chief function of the administrative jargons that appear in every bureaucratic organization.

Language Forms as Symbols

In every controversial political situation the tension between skepticism and loyalty constitutes a basic dimension of people's attitudes toward authorities and toward aspirants for power. Supplementing substantive argument and evidence as influences on these attitudes are the styles in which political discussion is carried on: the recurring resort to particular syntactic structures and ostensibly scientific terms that seem to be associated either with support of authority or with a critical and inquiring stance. Though everyday political language intermingles the two styles, it is possible to recognize some common forms of each and, somewhat speculatively, to identify the political consequences of each form and of their combination in everyday political discourse.

The Language of Participation
and the Language of Resistance

Language and gestures define low-status groups either as joint participants in policymaking or as in conflict with authority. The distinction is crucial, with consequences for public opposition to regimes and for compliance with rules. Those who get the least of what there is to get inevitably feel contradictory incentives: to play their expected parts in established institutions or to resist them on the ground that they are inequitable. The definition of people with little status as directly involved in making public policy discourages them from resisting and at the same time minimizes the likelihood that a wider public will perceive them as unfairly deprived. In this sense, the perception of problematic political action as participation in government engenders quiescence, while a focus on adversary interests encourages resistance.

Whether particular political actions are forms of participation or forms of conflict is ordinarily no more self-evident than whether basic interests are in conflict; the perception depends heavily on linguistic and gestural categorization. Were the representatives of the poor in the Community Action agencies maximum feasible participants or were the agencies one more forum for conflict with the establishment? It is hardly surprising that the decisions denying cherished values to large groups of people are often politicized, encouraging the perception that all interested parties were represented in their formulation.[1]

Political participation symbolizes influence for the powerless, but it is also a key device for social control. In consequence, liberals, radicals, and authoritarians all favor participation, a tribute to the term's symbolic potency and semantic hollowness.

Public and Private Issues

To politicize an issue is to define it as appropriate for public decision making: to take it for granted that people do not have the right to act autonomously and privately and to engender that belief in others. Politicization is the creation of a state of mind, whatever else it is. Which issues are seen as appropriate for private and which for public decision making is always dependent on social cueing. How workers are paid and treated on the job has been regarded as an employer prerogative at some times and places and has been politicized at others. The same problematic status holds for matters of faith and morals, and, indeed, for every form of human behavior.

Once made, the definition of an issue as either political or private in character is typically accepted by people who are not directly affected, though it usually remains controversial for those who are subjected to controls. Trade associations continue to try to modify laws regulating hours, wages, and working conditions; but the definition of welfare recipients as subject to administrative surveillance, of citizens as prohibited from seeing plays and movies defined as obscene, and of students as subject to specific controls by school authorities is generally taken for granted by the public unless active resistance makes them problematic. Organized groups with financial resources more easily mount resistance than do people subjected to constraints because of their poverty, their age, or their noncon-

---

[1] Herbert Simon explores the contribution of facts and values to administrative decision making in *Administrative Behavior*, 2nd ed. (New York: Macmillan, 1957), though he is not sensitive to the sense in which fact and value are empirically inseparable from each other and to the basic tautology.

formist behavior. The latter groups often accept the constraints as in their own interest, doubtless with considerable ambivalence.

Participation in public policymaking remains a central symbol of democracy, whether a particular instance of politicization extends personal influence or severely constricts it. Those who have lost their autonomy may be acutely aware of the fact or they may be ambivalent, for the symbol means democracy to them too; but for the public that is not directly involved, it is the democratic connotation of participation that prevails whenever the emphasis is upon "self-government."

The denial of personal autonomy through politicization of virtually all facets of life is the key device through which authoritarian governments control their populations, regardless of the prevailing ideology. Their forceful suppression of dissidents is more conspicuous and dramatic; but suppression brings disorder unless psychological controls win popular support for it; and politicization is psychologically effective because it is accepted as democratic. Participation in group meetings has often been obligatory: in China, in Russia, and in Nazi Germany, just as it usually is in mental hospitals, in prisons, and in high schools that emphasize student self-government; for it helps evoke popular acquiescence in rules that would be resisted if authorities imposed them by fiat.

Where bargaining resources are equal, participation produces real influence on who gets what. When they are strikingly unequal, as is almost always the case, participation becomes a *symbol* of influence that encourages quiescence, rather than substantive gains, for the powerless. Group decision making therefore produces predictable outcomes by reflecting existing inequalities in the resources of participants, especially their resources for influencing others to define the political world as they do. To put the point another way, politicization is likely to assure that decisions reflecting existing allocations of resources will be regarded as basically sound. It is less often the method of reaching decisions than the critical decision in itself.

Politicization as Co-optation

Even formal participation through representatives helps win acceptance of the dominant values of the organization or the polity. The German codetermination laws granting formal representation to workers in the management of plants have made worker representatives sensitive to the financial and managerial problems of the administrators and have not been the radical measures many assumed they would be when they were first enacted after World War II.[2] "Maximum feasible participation" of the poor in the American Community Action agencies has had much the same result; it has done little to increase the political influence of the poor.[3] Government departments and "regulatory" commissions reflect the interests of groups with large private resources with striking consistency.[4]

Totalitarian regimes recognize that public attendance at political discussions is an effective way to induce potential dissidents to conform to the dominant ideology, for group discussion enlists peer-group pressure, and peers are both more credible and less easily rejected than authorities, who continue to furnish the dominant values and the available "facts." For the same reasons coerced political participation, labeled self-government, patient government, or group therapy is invaluable to authorities in prisons, mental hospitals, and schools, and, to a smaller degree, in political discussion that is not coerced except through social pressure.

This nonobvious effect of politicization is certainly not its only effect. Where discontent is widespread, political discussion gives authorities information about the thresholds of deprivation beyond which disorder is likely, and so may limit deprivation. Participants may offer tactical suggestions, many of which are acceptable to authorities.

Policymaking bodies also resolve issues that pit different influential groups against one another.[5] Though such discussions may be critical for competing elites, they do not significantly affect most people's power or resources.

With these important exceptions, formal procedures and discussions are instances of ritual, not of policymaking, in the sense that

[2] Herbert Spiro, *The Politics of German Codetermination* (Cambridge, Mass.: Harvard University Press, 1958).

[3] Ralph M. Kramer, *Participation of the Poor: Comparative Case Studies in the War on Poverty* (Englewood Cliffs, N.J.: Prentice-Hall, 1969), pp. 244–50.

[4] See Murray Edelman, *The Symbolic Uses of Politics* (Urbana: University of Illinois Press, 1964), chaps. 2 and 3.

[5] Thomas R. Dye and L. Harmon Ziegler, *The Irony of Democracy* (Belmont, Cal.: Wadsworth, 1970).

they influence popular beliefs and perceptions while purporting, usually falsely, to be directly influencing events and behavior. A rain dance is a ritual for the same reason. Formal governmental procedures, in whatever setting they take place, *are* formalities, vital for inducing general acquiescence in power arrangements.

Influence versus Formality

It is those who can exercise influence *outside* the context of formal proceedings who wield real power. Political influence flows from the employment of resources that shape the beliefs and behavior of others. Common resources include expert skills, the restriction of information, the ability to confer favors on others or to injure them, physical force, and subtle or crude bribery. Examples are business lobbying, the influence of economists and statisticians on tax legislation, legislative logrolling, corporate price fixing, shared values among industries and the officials charged with their regulation, and the esteem authorities, professionals, and much of the public accord to wealth and high social status.

Such resources influence all significant decisions of governmental and other authoritative institutions, though formal proceedings must legitimize them. The knowledgeable politician, lawyer, professional, or analyst becomes successful by using his or her knowledge of informal influence, though even these experts often see policy as made in formal settings when they are addressing a high school commencement, rather than lobbying or plea bargaining. As discussion groups function, legislation is enacted, court cases heard and decided, and administrative regulations formally considered and promulgated, background understandings and informal processes instill values and information that determine the outcome. These processes may be embedded in rituals, but they are not themselves ritualistic, for they directly account for actions that allocate resources. Behind the administrator's, the politician's, and the professional's formal recommendations and decisions lie his or her group ties and understandings with interest groups. Behind the votes and speeches of rank-and-file members of policymaking bodies lie their expectations of social approval or censure and their fears of sanctions. Both the publicized and the unpublicized aspects of policymaking processes have functions to serve—the former chiefly ritualistic, the latter chiefly influential in shaping value allocations. ITT influences a great many governmental policies without formal participation, while a member of a "therapeutic community" participates all day without significantly changing policy outcomes. Those who have the resources are influential without the need for formal participation, and those who lack them can use participation only to share in formulating policies that reflect their weakness.

The argument that the most publicized and cherished governmental procedures are largely ritualistic is self-evidently based on an evaluative judgment, as all classifications are. Formal procedures are ritualistic in the sense that they will not effect any basic or radical change in existing inequalities in wealth or power. They will certainly yield many policies that have symbolic effects and they may effect minor changes in income or tax policies, usually in response to economic conditions already influencing such trends. Socialization and symbolic processes lead a great many people to define such marginal change as significant. Those who favor it portray it as substantial, for their political careers as well as their self-conceptions hinge on that belief. Their conclusion, like its opposite, is manifestly a value judgment: Politicization systematically masks public recognition that the outcomes of formal procedures are largely symbolic or marginal in character. Without such masking, resort to these procedures by the poor would obviously be less uncritical and reliance on the influence conferred by their numbers through direct political action more common.

The Uses of Disorder

Nonelites, and especially the poor, lack the informal sanctions and other resources that confer influence, with the important exception that if they act together, they can create disorder and in that way threaten elites. They rarely do so because in becoming politicized, mass publics implicitly renounce disorder as a political weapon. To accept an issue as appropriate for political decision making is to define it as inappropriate for an open power confrontation. Because the political power of the poor stems ultimately only from the possibility of collective action that interferes with established routines, politicization minimizes their power, substituting ritualistic participation or representation. The consequences of this exchange are not obvious, though they are potent. Politicization can be taken as a signal that nonelites have renounced resort to disorder and that substantial concessions are not necessary.

People do sometimes resort to passive resistance, riot, rebellion, or economic strikes that are something more than a temporary change in the form of collective bargaining about incremental gains. These cases underline the point just made about conventional politics, for they are either suppressed by greater force or they succeed in winning substantial concessions. Through disorder the poor have increased welfare benefits in the United States and have liberalized eligibility provisions.[6] The French, American, Russian, and English revolutions exemplify more dramatic uses of collective power to win major concessions.

Mass disorder wins substantial concessions when it threatens the privileges of elites or disrupts programs on which they rely. Public protest, peaceful and violent, has repeatedly won wide support by forcing public attention to shocking conditions and grievances that had been ignored as long as political participation remained conventional and ritualistic. In these circumstances, disorder may create ambivalence even among authorities and economic elites, further contributing to the likelihood of concessions.

Disorder invites repression when potential allies see the tactics of protest as more shocking than the grievances to which the protesters try to call public attention; and it invites a response that is only tokenistic or symbolic when the protest is narrow in scope and expressed through conventional tactics, such as demonstrations or strikes of a kind that occur routinely to express discontent.[7] But whether a supportive or a symbolic response or a backlash occurs is itself influenced by the evocative forms already discussed.[8] Politicization is the most common and the most effective of these.

[6] Frances F. Piven and Richard A. Cloward, *Regulating the Poor* (New York: Vintage, 1971), chap. 1.

[7] Michael Lipsky, "Protest as a Political Resource," *American Political Science Review* 62 (December 1968): 1144–58.

[8] I have discussed the political and symbolic processes that win or alienate mass support in Murray Edelman, *Politics as Symbolic Action* (New York: Academic Press, 1971).

The Structuring of Perception
through Politicization

Because participation symbolizes democracy, it systematically clouds recognition of conflicting interests that persist regardless of negotiation. The adoption of formal procedures for direct or indirect participation in decisions conveys the message that differences stem from misunderstandings that can be clarified through discussion or that they deal with preferences that are readily compromised. For reasons already discussed, such routines perpetuate and legitimize existing inequalities in influence, in the application of law, and in the allocation of values.

A large body of empirical and theoretical work demonstrates that the impact of the most widely publicized formal governmental policies is consistently small or symbolic, especially when both proponents and opponents expect the policies in question to mark a substantial change. This generalization holds for civil rights legislation, business regulation, welfare policy, housing policy, and every other important area of domestic governmental action.[9]

The extant research on policy outcomes and on the shaping of cognitions suggests that politicization focuses public attention on incremental change while masking perception of the inequalities underlying the increments. A tough legislative battle over an 8 percent increase in welfare benefits gives the combatants and their supporters a sense of victory or defeat that minimizes attention to persisting poverty and gross inequalities in living standards. Public disorder, by contrast, occasionally succeeds in drawing public attention to social inequalities while it minimizes appreciation of incremental change.

Intense Politicization

Especially intense forms of politicization are imposed on people who challenge the legitimacy of the established order by breaking the law or by practicing or advocating other forms of behavior perceived as too threatening or too unconventional to tolerate. Offenses

[9] See Kenneth Dolbeare, "The Impacts of Public Policies," *American Government Annual*, 1974.

against property constitute the most direct challenge, but actions that symbolize rejection of their beliefs about proper behavior offend supporters of the established order even more than individual delinquency does. Unconventional language, dress, and manners and unconventional sexual, religious, and political practices and beliefs have repeatedly brought demands for their forceful suppression or their definition as sickness requiring rehabilitation. Because the conventional find it intolerable to accept such behaviors as legitimate alternatives to their own moral codes, they welcome their definition as individual deviance. This categorization wins popular support for their suppression, by force or by peer pressure, while it denies that the suppression is political in character.

In schools, welfare agencies, prisons, and mental hospitals, people labeled deviant are subjected, often involuntarily, to group therapy, inmate meetings, and discussions with social workers and psychiatrists. The "deviants" are overwhelmingly poor people who have violated legal norms or other social conventions; the remainder are people who are unwilling or unable to adapt to their worlds and the roles they are constrained to play. Through group discussion they are encouraged to define their problems as personal, and as remediable through adjustment to conventions. They are encouraged to see the group discussions as a form of democratic participation and therapy rather than as social pressure for individual conformity. Whatever its clinical uses may be, such participation is an intensive mode of blurring the perception that the interests of clients and authorities are adversary in some key respects and of inducing people to substitute personal adaptation to their circumstances for dissenting politics, an adversary posture, or a test of power.

That the professional staff and a large part of the clientele accept such discussions as a form of self-government, even though attendance is typically compulsory, is a revealing instance of the ambivalence of cognitions. Both staff and inmates recognize, indeed assert, that the meetings are a part of a program for curbing deviance; and they also recognize, though not so explicitly, that the staff narrowly limits the agenda to be discussed and decided and that only minor variations from staff preferences are tolerated in the decisions the group can make. Yet the *forms* of democratic participation and the belief that inmates are governing themselves coexist with recognition that the forms restrict participants. Forms generate one set of cognitions and content an inconsistent set. The mind readily entertains both, cued by changing settings and signals to express one or the other.

This phenomenon is easy to see in small groups, and it throws light on the same phenomenon when it occurs in the larger polity; for the poor and the discontented are constantly exposed to the same kind of ambivalence so far as most governmental social and economic policies are concerned. They resent repressive taxes, inadequate and degrading welfare benefits, military drafts that ensure that the poor sacrifice most,[10] educational systems that provide the least effective schooling for the poor, and police forces that give the poor the least protection and the most harassment. At the same time, they generally accept all these policies and many others that are discriminatory because they are the end products of a democratic system the public is socialized to support. In these cases, too, the form and the content of governmental actions generate inconsistent cognitive structures. The reassuring forms are almost always the more powerful component, partly because they affect everyone, while resentment against particular policies is confined to narrower groupings, dividing people because they focus on different grievances. The lower-middle-class worker who resents his or her tax bill may have little sympathy for the unemployed black who pays no taxes and resents his or her treatment at the welfare office.

Discussion groups formally charged with decisions affecting their members always operate within the context of a larger organization dominated by authorities who can offer greater rewards and impose more severe penalties than the discussion group itself. In this situation the "self-governing" groups can almost always be counted on to stay well within the limits acceptable to authority and to discourage nonconformist thought and behavior more severely than the authorities can do it. As already noted, authorities must be anxious about appearing to be despotic, a concern that peers using democratic forms need not share.

There are always some participants who assume the role of guardians of the established rules, conventions, and morality and zealously suppress unconventional thought and behavior. Because inmates who dislike or resent discussions and this form of "self-government" withdraw or remain passive, those in the guardian role dominate

[10] James Davis and Kenneth Dolbeare, *Little Groups of Neighbors* (Chicago: Markham, 1968).

meetings and influence members who vacillate. The assumption of the role of guardian may stem from agreement with the rules, from fear, or from the hope of personal privilege; but the role is invariably filled, so that the establishment of inmate self-government is a safe course for authorities charged with controlling the behavior of students, mental patients, or prison inmates.

Because the guardian role is an acting out of the expectations of the dominant groups in a society, it is hardly surprising that it consistently appears among low-status people, even where the guardians openly curb groups of which they themselves are members. To cite some polar cases, the role was fulfilled in the American slave plantations [11] and in the Nazi extermination camps,[12] and it is conspicuous in enlisted men's army barracks and among black policemen assigned to urban ghettos. While these are hardly examples of self-government, even in ritualistic form, they do exemplify the universality, in every polity, with which some respond to the expectations of dominant authority.

The role appears as well in representative governmental bodies, including legislatures, administrative agencies, and courts,[13] and in these settings it represents a built-in conservative bias. Obviously, the bias is weaker in representative bodies than in total institutions and dictatorships, where the power of the authorities is more conspicuous and the occasions and purpose of its exercise more predictable. Occupants of the role doubtless feel ambivalent about playing it, and those who refuse to assume it may feel some temptation to do so. Though authorities and the guardians that support them must often deny widely supported demands, the setting in which they act and the participation of representatives of the people blurs the adversary character of their actions; and blurring widens the freedom of action of the authorities.

The ambivalent willingness of people to subject themselves to dominant authority and to renounce autonomy has often been recognized by social psychologists and political scientists and is perhaps

[11] Stanley M. Elkins, *Slavery: A Problem in American Institutional and Intellectual Life* (New York: Grosset and Dunlap, 1963).

[12] Hannah Arendt, *Eichmann in Jerusalem: A Report on the Banality of Evil* (London: Faber, 1963).

[13] Ralph K. Huitt, "The Outsider in the Senate: An Alternative Role," *American Political Science Review* 55 (September 1961): 566–75; Murray Edelman, *The Symbolic Uses of Politics*, chap. 3.

most sensitively analyzed by Erich Fromm.[14] It is easy but inaccurate to see such willingness as characteristic of particular personality types, such as "authoritarian personalities," rather than of human beings in general when they are anxious about contingencies they cannot control. The disposition to "escape from freedom" is bound to be a significant element in groups that substitute collective decision making for individual action and personal responsibility. By the same token, submission to a group and to authority doubtless is comforting to many anxious and discontented people, helping them to resolve their personal frustrations and indecision. Group discussion obviously holds clinical benefits for some, but my interest is in its political implications.

Research in milieu and therapeutic communities supports these conclusions about the conservative and ritualistic character of meetings formally labeled self-government. One of the few psychiatrists to examine such meetings as political phenomena concludes that the self-government is in fact "pseudodemocracy." The staff continues to manage the agenda of the meetings and to control them by bringing pressure on susceptible patients to support particular rules; and inmates' decisions are ignored when the staff dislikes them.

The same study found that in self-governing psychiatric communities there is a marked increase in mood and morale shifts among both patients and staff.[15] The frequent shifts in mood and morale are evidence of the significant psychological pressure the meetings exert, a phenomenon that is hardly consistent either with its portrayal as a forum for inmate influence or with the assumption that it is bound to be therapeutic, unless health is defined as political con-

[14] Erich Fromm, *Escape from Freedom* (New York: Farrar, Strauss, and Giroux, 1944).

[15] James R. Greenley, "Types of Authority and Two Problems of Psychiatric Wards," *Psychiatric Quarterly* 47 (1973): 191–202. Another study that reached much the same conclusions is Ben Bursten, "Decision-Making in the Hospital Community," *Archives of General Psychiatry* 29 (December 1973): 732–35. See also Robert Rubenstein and Harold D. Lasswell, *The Sharing of Power in a Psychiatric Hospital* (New Haven: Yale University Press, 1966). For a report of a study that found that milieu therapy and individual psychotherapy are the "least effective, most expensive, and most time consuming" forms of psychiatric treatment see Arnold A. Rogow, *The Psychiatrists* (London: George Allen and Unwin, 1970), p. 201.

formity. As Goffman has noted of mental hospitals and Cicourel of schools,[16] there is no place one can be free of surveillance and pressure, no place to hide, very little independence; and the involvement of fellow inmates in the surveillance and the pressure intensifies both. In this sense self-government in its ritualistic form constitutes an extension of the bureaucratization of everyday life. What is called self-government in total institutions comes close to denying all autonomous influence to inmates.

The staff provides the values and the methods for inmate meetings. The fundamental decision, that personal and civil liberties individuals value may be abridged, is a staff policy and cannot be reversed. The "participation" amounts to help in *enforcing* staff rules, not in making policy. Almost all of the participation, in fact, consists of legitimizing deprivations for those participants whose status is low. Just as the formal representatives of workers on wage control agencies make rules limiting wage demands their fellow workers would otherwise be free to back with strike action if necessary, so inmates of total institutions spend their time in self-government meetings making rules that deny their fellow inmates civil rights other citizens enjoy automatically. Formal participation by low-status groups categorizes denial of benefits and denial of bargaining power as a form of influence.

One virtually universal staff principle also springs from problematic categorization: the definition of civil rights and elementary personal freedoms as "privileges." A psychiatrist who experimented with alternative terms has observed that:

> Thinking in terms of *privilege,* the staff looks at it as reward, something extra, something to be earned. . . . We may hardly have any feelings about "withholding privileges" . . . they just have not been "earned yet," or the patient "doesn't deserve them." Thinking in terms of *rights* changes the whole picture. We hesitate to deprive people of their rights, or we feel less benevolent when we restore them. I have seen some marked changes in attitude on my own ward when the terminology has been altered.[17]

[16] Erving Goffman, *Asylums* (Garden City, N.Y.: Anchor, 1961), p. xiii; Aaron V. Cicourel and John I. Kitsuse, *The Educational Decision-Makers* (Indianapolis: Bobbs-Merrill, 1963).

[17] Bursten, "Decision-Making in the Hospital Community," p. 733.

The same writer, basing his conclusions on observations in three hospitals, found a sharp decrease in tension, a more relaxed atmosphere among patients, and much less frequent crises when the pretense of self-government was abandoned and patients were routinely accorded their civil rights.

There are some revealing analogies in assumptions, in emphasis, and in concepts between the institutions that reflect the psychiatric ideology and the Nazi German state, and these point to common psychological processes that underlie both forms of polity. In calling attention to these analogies I do not imply that the two are morally analogous or that these forms of control cannot be defended in psychiatric institutions, though I would not defend them. My interest lies in tracing their similar influence on political cognition and behavior.

These analogies are conspicuous:

1. clear hierarchies of competence and merit, with most of the population consigned to the lowest category and assumed to require strong guidance and control by authority, who alone can decide on policy directions;
2. definition of all individual activities as public in character and of privacy as suspect and unhealthy;
3. discouragement of individuality and concomitant emphasis on adaptation to the community and respect for authority, which is assumed to embody the true will of the community;
4. denigration of the intellect as promoting divisiveness, mistakes, disorder, and confusion;
5. a strong focus on feeling, especially on the evocation of feelings shared with others;
6. frequent employment of the metaphor of health and sickness in defining people's psychological and moral condition, with the mass public assumed to be either sick or in constant danger of infection, but capable of improvement through diligent performance of established roles;
7. a consequent emphasis on purity, expressed in specific puritanical restrictions on personal conduct;
8. a strong focus on the need for security against an enemy who is all the more dangerous because he *looks* normal and harmless: the Jew or the Communist, the parent or the culture of poverty that produces deviance;

9. readiness to employ force to ensure the victory of healthy forces over diseased ones: involuntary preventive detention, modification or destruction of the sick person or personality.

Inculcation of this pattern of assumptions and cognitions produces the ultimate degree of compliance with established norms and authority and the strongest insurance against the adoption of an adversary political posture of self-assertion, of independence, or of skepticism. At the same time, it engenders the form of mass contentment and security Fromm identified, for it lulls the critical faculties and discourages autonomy. The various components of the pattern manifestly reinforce each other; and they are compatible with an emphasis upon a public language. The contentment and security the pattern produces are therefore certain to be short-lived; for the life to which it adapts people is possible only in a contrived environment that is virtually all ritual in its social forms and that makes independent inquiry difficult. Because errors are unlikely to be detected or corrected, effective action is impossible for long.

Obviously, formal participation in such a setting has far more intensive and repressive policy effects and psychological consequences than it has in democratic policymaking institutions in which social stratification is blurred, intelligence welcomed, and a considerable measure of independence encouraged. In the latter case, independent research and information from nongovernmental sources can be influential in shaping policy directions, and informal modes of influence on policy reinforce personal assertiveness and independence. What is alike about the two settings is the effect of formal proceedings. In both cases these encourage acceptance of dominant perceptions and beliefs; but in authoritarian institutions only formal authorities are permitted to function outside the ambit of formal proceedings.

Clarification and Blurring of Adversary Relations

For authorities and dominant social groups, political situations that call attention to adversary interests and to the forms of power available to the interested groups are risky. Forceful suppression and open resistance are the polar cases. The employment of force to suppress resistance or dissent engenders fears of the arbitrary and despotic use of power. It encourages popular opposition that threatens to curb or overthrow the regime unless the repression is reinforced by psychological ploys that lend it legitimacy. Resort to force to suppress dissent is therefore a clear signal that a regime is unstable and limited in what it can do, precisely because forceful suppression of others symbolizes unlimited power.

In both its general and its intensive forms politicization has the opposite effect on public opinion. By focusing on popular participation, by clouding recognition of adversary interests, by presenting authorities as helping and rehabilitative, it symbolizes the constriction of elite power within narrow limits. Public attention then focuses on procedures rather than on their outcomes, so that the power to coerce, degrade, and confuse dissidents is greater.

Involvement in situations that are openly adversary in character heightens the self-esteem of people with low status: those defined as inadequate, incompetent, deviant, or subservient. More likely, heightened self-esteem and heightened willingness to assert one's rights are expressions of each other. In the England of the early nineteenth century [18] and in the United States of the thirties, the industrial worker who first took part in open conflict with his or her employer typically exhibited a new self-respect and felt a new dignity. Frantz Fanon concludes that the open resistance of African colonials to continued rule by the European powers similarly brought a more autonomous personality into being.[19]

Differences exist among total institutions in the degree to which people define the staff–inmate relationship as adversary. In prisons, the power relationship is clear; inmates and guards typically see their interests as largely adversary in character; and so subordination is very largely a function of coercion. The prisoner does not have to internalize his subordinate status in the form of a belief that he deserves his subservience and is benefiting from it. To a smaller degree and in a more ambivalent way, the same is true of the relationship of students and teachers in the public schools, especially in the ghettos, where schooling is more openly a form of custody

---

[18] E. P. Thompson, *The Making of the English Working Class* (London: Penguin, 1964), chap. 11.

[19] Frantz Fanon, *The Wretched of the Earth* (London: MacGibbon and Kee, 1965).

than it is in middle-class neighborhoods. The movement to make psychiatric and social-work counseling a part of prison and school programs amounts politically to a blurring of the power relationship and encouragement to internalize the norms of authorities; but it is doubtful that it has been very effective in achieving this aim; for the locus of power is clear, and both prisoners and students easily establish informal alliances among themselves, which thereby win some concessions and also underline the adversary relationship. While rituals of subordination and of self-government may be imposed, they are recognized as tests of physical power, and only rarely as evidence of intellectual or moral worth.

The case is different with welfare recipients and inmates of psychiatric institutions. Early socialization inculcates the belief that these are helping institutions for the inadequate, and staff procedures reinforce that perception, even though welfare recipients and patients are likely to develop considerable ambivalence about it. Hospitalized mental patients are more ready to define one another as intellectually and morally inadequate and therefore to yield to staff pressure to help control one another, rather than forming alliances to confront authorities. Welfare recipients normally do not meet one another in a way that permits them to form alliances. When a leadership springs up that encourages alliance, as in the Welfare Rights Organization, the result *is* more self-respect and confidence and a measure of power to extract concessions from authorities.

Mortification rituals reinforce subordination and individual isolation: deprivation of ordinary civil rights and the requirement of confession of abnormalities in mental patients, need tests, submission to bureaucratic probing into their private lives, and long waits in demoralizing settings for welfare recipients. The basic fact, however, is that the power relationship is blurred, and this in turn wins general public support for the authorities while minimizing the incentive of the "helped" clienteles to assert their rights or to behave like adversaries.

It is symptomatic of this difference in the recognition of adversary interests and power that the rapidly increasing use of involuntary behavior modification is being militantly resisted in prisons on the ground that it represses and brutalizes prisoners under the guise of science; but there is little resistance to it in mental hospitals, where it is used more widely and its methods and political consequences are similar.

Though there are important analogies to the larger polity, and I have called attention to some of them, much of this discussion focuses on the forms politicization takes in institutions that deal with children and with people who have conspicuously failed to conform to accepted conventions. These institutions play a central role in the larger polity, all the more important because it is usually unrecognized or minimized. Most of the population behaves within acceptable limits as a result of ordinary socialization processes, with no need for intensive politicization. Yet the conspicuous labeling and segregation of some as "deviants" constitutes a potent, though masked and subtle, reinforcement of conventional thought and behavior. Those who are so labeled serve as a benchmark for everyone, marking off normality from unacceptability. In this sense politicization in total institutions underlies and reinforces the norms that find overt expression in the entire polity.

Antipolitics

The perception of an issue as nonpolitical often serves to win general acceptance for elite values, just as politicization does, even though the two categorizations are nominally dichotomous. The definition of a decision as professional or technical in character justifies decision making by professionals and technicians and promotes mass acceptance of their conclusions. It therefore avoids the need for ritualized political meetings and minimizes the likelihood of mass protest or disorder.

As symbolic processes, politicization and antipolitics reinforce each other, for both induce mass quiescence while leaving the critical tactics for influencing policy to groups that can employ special resources in money, skills, and public esteem. A population socialized from infancy to believe it is incompetent to deal with the important decisions because they are technical and complex is the more satisfied with ritualistic participation that stays within the limits set by professional and governmental authorities and which serves chiefly to induce conformity. Whenever a political issue threatens to produce conflict or an impasse or a result unacceptable to elites, some will define and perceive it as inappropriate for politics: as calling for specialized expertise rather than political negotiation and compromise. There is always a good deal of receptivity throughout the population to this way of defining a difficult issue, for it allows people who are worried but baffled by a problem to believe that those who know best will deal with it.

Few like to live a politicized life, and that is probably a good thing. Other values are more important to most of us than political participation. We would rather make love than war, rather read literature, ski, play pool, or make pottery than discuss urban zoning or international trade agreements. At the same time, we are anxiously aware that political decisions can affect our lives profoundly and even end them. A common consequence of this combination of deep concern and lack of interest in detailed participation is eagerness to accept those who present themselves as knowledgeable and who are willing to make political decisions. Because acceptance of the leader or authority who supposedly knows how to cope is so largely based on eagerness to ignore politics, it is understandable that authoritative decisions are usually accepted for long periods, regardless of their consequences. The authority's charisma, stemming from his or her dramaturgy of coping with anxiety-producing problems, is what focuses public attention, not the impacts of the policies, which are difficult to know, even after detailed study.

Consider some of the "problems" in which the critical decisions are routinely made so as to exclude the most seriously affected groups from influence. Until a new militancy about highway location emerged in recent years, highway engineers regularly concluded that city expressways could most economically be built through the neighborhoods in which the poor live, thereby destroying the communities that are important to the poor and depriving them of low-cost housing. But it was accepted that this kind of decision should be based chiefly on engineering considerations; and engineers learn in school how to calculate costs. The denial to the poor of influence proportionate to their suffering from such policies is legitimized for many, including many of the poor themselves, by defining the issue as professional. To most of the middle class who are aware that there is an "issue," the rationality of the process is self-evident and the costs to the poor invisible. The designation of the issue as "professional" or "technical" is manifestly metaphoric, for it highlights one of its aspects while masking others; but the metaphor evokes or reinforces a cognitive structure in the individual and a dominant public opinion in the polity.

Public officials regularly reconstruct their behavior and their motives in order to legitimize their actions in terms that will bring broad public support. Piven and Cloward have shown, for example, that welfare rolls expand when social disorder increases and contract when the authorities recognize they can cut people off from welfare without fear of further disorder.[20] Both legislative and administrative decisions to expand or contract the number of welfare recipients are inevitably justified, however, in terms of professional judgments of need. If disorder is mentioned in rhetoric, it is almost always to *deny* that the authorities will yield to "violent and illegitimate demands." The rhetoric manifestly serves to win support, not to describe the grounds for decision making.

Increasingly, public officials cite their specialized knowledge and the need for expert planning as reason to exclude from politics the very decisions that impinge most heavily on public well-being. Neither the public nor Congress can be trusted to decide when to wage war or escalate it because only the executive has the special intelligence to know such things. Foreign policy in general should be above politics. Urban planning is for urban planners, not for the people who live in cities, and especially not for those who live in central cities rather than suburbs.

Notice that it is the categorization of these problems that legitimizes the power of specialized authorities to deal with them, even though their decisions systematically affect many other aspects of people's lives. Military planners create employment in some places, unemployment in others, inflation everywhere, and moral dilemmas in many; but the problem is labeled "military." Psychiatrists reinforce the norm that cheerful adjustment to poverty or war or a constricted life is healthy while despondency or anger in the face of these pathologies is sick; but their decisions are labeled "medical."

In the contemporary world, a governmental decision is likely to have severe effects on many aspects of our lives, not upon only one or a few. For this reason the labeling of policies as "military" or "medical" is both metaphoric and metonymic. It stands for a larger pattern of cognitions or it highlights a similarity to something familiar while masking other critical features. In doing so, it legitimizes a specific kind of political authority while masking the pertinence of other interests.

Anxiety about foreign enemies, internal subversion, and deviant

---

[20] Piven and Cloward, *Regulating the Poor.*

behavior is especially widespread and is frequently reinforced by government officials. Military, police, and psychiatric authorities benefit most consistently from this form of linguistic structuring. Anxiety about economic survival and social problems, by contrast, is limited to particular groups, is far more sporadic, and is constantly deflated by governmental claims that the outlook is good. Every regime thinks it is politically essential to claim that its economic and social policies are working successfully, even while it reinforces fears of foreign and internal enemies. In consequence, economic and social deprivations that flow from decisions classified as "military," "security," or "rehabilitative" are more readily concealed from mass publics through metaphor. Such systematic inflation of the forms of threat that legitimize authority and systematic deflation of the forms of threat that legitimize domestic redistribution of goods and influence inevitably has consequences for the effectiveness of public policies. It diverts resources toward coping with mythical threats and makes it unlikely that the problems of nonelites will be effectively confronted.

Political Constraint through Symbolic Reassurance

Governments sometimes solve social problems or minimize the harm they do. Public programs also accomplish impressive engineering feats, achieve scientific breakthroughs, and help victims of natural disasters. Effective political action is likely when it does not disturb power, income, or status hierarchies. More often, politics creates a way of living with social problems by defining them as inevitable or as equitable.

Though poverty and many other serious problems are obviously chronic, the language in which officials and the general public routinely discuss them focuses attention on the formal goal of overcoming them and masks many of the results of public policies. Denial

Parts of this chapter are from Murray Edelman, "On Policies That Fail," *The Progressive* 39 (May 1975): 22–23. Used by permission from *The Progressive*, 408 West Gorham Street, Madison, Wisconsin 53703. Copyright © 1975, The Progressive, Inc.

of money, status, and influence to the poor is attributed to human nature, to economic laws, or to the inevitable imperfection of government, even while the dignity of the person is affirmed and the victimization of the powerless deplored. Such evocation of multiple realities has profound, if nonobvious, consequences for politics. It encourages both the powerful and the powerless to accept their situations while permitting both to express their abhorrence of poverty and their dedication to reform. The result is the continuation of broad public support for recurrent policies regardless of their empirical consequences. Ambivalence in the individual, ambiguity in political situations, and contradictory beliefs about problems and authorities reinforce one another whenever governments deal with controversial issues. Yet prevailing symbols and ideology depict public policy as a rational conversion of popular "wants" into policies that normally solve public problems, with occasional defects in the process. Everyone is susceptible to that symbolization and socialization; popular talk, recurring political rhetoric, and sophisticated political theorizing all reflect it.

It can be overcome, as the phenomenologists have taught us, only by a more rigorous empiricism than conventional social science teaches: by self-conscious suspension of the assumptions about people's capacities and motives that ordinarily color our observations, and by observation of behavior in the worlds people inhabit in their everyday lives, rather than in the "reality" the man in the street and the conventional social scientist have been taught to take for granted when they talk about government. With such suspension of background assumptions, an observer begins to recognize that it is *language* about political events rather than the events themselves that everyone experiences; that the unintended consequences of actions and language are often more important than the intended ones; and that conventional observation and conventional research methods (notably opinion and attitude research) chiefly tell us which symbols are currently powerful, not what "reality" is. To define the cognitive effects of symbols as people's "wants" is to justify institutions and policies, not to explain their genesis or dynamics.

Poverty is the preeminent example of problematic symbolization, as is only to be expected of the condition that epitomizes inequality in wealth, in quality of life, and in political power. Part of the dubious categorization of poverty involves defining as its causes what social scientists commonly see as its consequences: physical and mental handicaps, crime, lack of ambition, and business cycle fluctuations. The contradictory views coexist because the commonplace perception of cause and effect in a complex social situation depends on what is taken for granted, not on what can be verified or falsified. Symbols subtly evoke assumptions and cognitive structures.

If the consequences of *poverty* are problematic, the consequences of its problematic *categorization* are not. Dubious definitions of poverty engender beliefs about which people are competent and deserve esteem and influence and which are incompetent and require regulation; about which governmental actions are helpful and which damaging—all dependent for their premises on social cueing rather than observation. Contradictory structures of perception and belief make it easy to support policies that serve one's interests and to still doubts and qualms by shifting among beliefs as cues and situations change. Largely unconscious structuring processes produce firm opinions either way: one reality that justifies existing inequalities and another one that justifies changes to minimize or erase poverty.

By recognizing the tie between *how* men and women perceive and *what* they perceive we can understand some political phenomena that are typically unnoticed. Only respecting public affairs do people exhibit so bewildering an amalgam of effective calculation on the one hand and of delusion, persistent error, and unresolved controversy over fundamental facts on the other. Just as the poor, legal offenders, emotionally disturbed people, and rebels are both victims and villains, so also are corporate managers, "the best and the brightest" who launch policies that fail tragically, and everyone else who becomes a role. To see all failures as exceptions to a generally viable political "system" is both a reassuring response and an ideology. It masks recognition that delusion and error are at least as frequent and as "systematic" as success.

Governmental action always depends on popular acquiescence or resistance. But myth personifies consequences, attributing good or bad outcomes to particular individuals who symbolize success or failure. Myth substitutes heroes and villains for complicated social interactions, providing ready "explanations" that are popular because they offer an outlet for anger or for satisfaction without criticizing the institutions that give people their roles, even when those institutions yield policies that fail.

The Generation of Belief and of Skepticism

Dogmatic beliefs about problematic issues are the crucial cognitive outcome of political symbols. People who are sure that conventional political beliefs are fact support authority uncritically, while those who remain aware of the dubious foundation of conventional perceptions and beliefs are an irritant and a challenge to authorities. Personal anxiety and ambiguous issues engender political certainty, while a focus on specific objectives and the costs of achieving them stimulates the tentative postures and the willingness to challenge dogma that characterize any scientific enterprise.

Cognitive structures about political affairs are scientifically intriguing, and may be politically illusory, because everyone is susceptible both to symbolism and to the scientific attitude. To see susceptibility to misleading symbolism as either the exceptional case or as characteristic only of pathological types is itself a political judgment, for it rationalizes repression and unequal value allocations while masking evidence that both untenable beliefs and healthy skepticism characterize everyone, at least occasionally.

Several psychological processes analyzed earlier can now be recognized as functioning together to justify widely held political interests and role structures. The basic processes are: personification of fears and hopes, so that particular public figures symbolize them; perception of real human beings as objects; condensation of diverse issues and observations into a single symbol, promoting cognitive confusion; categorizations that unconsciously evoke elaborate structures of dogmatic belief; and resort to one set of cognitions to justify conforming behavior and to a contradictory set to rationalize the failure of authorities to achieve their goals.

Clearly, these psychological processes complement and reinforce one another. Leaders and other authorities come to symbolize fears or hopes. The poor, the rich, the discontented, offenders against conventionality or law, and other vaguely defined groups of people come to symbolize threats to the good life or victimization by elites, sickness or health, competence or inadequacy. The symbols commonly justify established authorities and their policies while also rationalizing inequalities, deprivations, and ineffective courses of action.

The Constriction of Perception

Should discontented individuals and groups participate in public affairs, withdraw from them, or resist the regime in power? This strategy question is classic; and it is equally classic for authorities to try to predetermine the choice by defining the alternatives for the discontented. Regimes that hope to erase or control dissent through cooperation equate participation with influence and define non-participation (lack of influence) as the only alternative. For ordinary citizens, appeals to vote and to work for a major party and the definition of meaningless or tokenistic policies as significant achievements serve this purpose. For people thought likely to express discontent actively, participation in the "government" of a mental ward, a prison wing, or other authoritarian institution is offered as a generous alternative to exclusion from influence. In both cases, resistance is defined as beyond the pale—as evidence of irrationality, evil, or susceptibility to undesirable influences. Though resistance is the only strategy that has historically brought influence to low-status populations, it is cognitively erased from serious consideration in all but the rare political situation.

The same linguistic and psychological processes constrict other political perceptions. To offer "help" to the poor is to perceive the alternative as no help, thereby winning general support for marginal welfare measures that are often constricting as well. But failure to help is never the real alternative. Help must be offered, at least in token form, to avoid resistance or rebellion. The alternative is to give the destitute and the powerless the autonomy and the economic power to fend for themselves without the need for dubious forms of "help"; but that policy entails the kind of reordering of status, wealth, and institutions that regimes routinely define as unrealistic, unworkable, and unfair.

Similarly, the demands of authorities for "loyalty" are always presented as though the alternative were disloyalty, usually with the implicit or explicit assumption that serious opposition to incumbent officials is disloyalty to the nation. This definition of the issue masks the alternative officials find most threatening: an independent stance that encourages skeptical examination of issues and governmental performance.

In the same way, official actions that purport to pursue popular goals are defined as though the alternative were refusal to give the public what it wants. Authorities always expect credit for their symbolic objectives regardless of their actual accomplishments: for a "war on poverty" that does relatively little to reduce poverty; for educating the young, even though the children of the poor get more boredom and indoctrination than education; for treating the mentally ill, when a high proportion of the "treatment" consists of conditioning the unconventional to conform. The real alternative to symbolic official actions is not denial of popular goals but their achievement in practice as well as in rhetoric. The linguistic constriction of perception blurs recognition of alternative possibilities.

The Political Viability of Unsuccessful Policies

A regime can continue indefinitely to pursue policies that deny most of the population what they are promised and what they value; yet public support for such policies typically continues in spite of the occasional repudiation of individual officials whose performance becomes inept enough that they become symbols of arrogance or corruption. It cannot be taken for granted that support for public officials depends on their performance in office.

Consider the range of areas in which the American government has for many years pursued courses of action that deny the values its policies are supposed to achieve. In foreign policy, every administration promises peace, repeatedly declares that its actions are zealously directed toward that end, protests its dedication to disarmament, and periodically voices the expectation that the marathon disarmament talks will soon succeed. This rhetoric is responsive to deep fears of war and hopes for peace. Yet the disarmament conferences do not disarm and the defense budget takes a major share of national appropriations at the insistence of the same officials who dedicate themselves to peace. The Pentagon's hard sell of large quantities of arms to foreign countries supplies weapons to both combatants in virtually every war except the frequent ones in which the United States is a combatant, and even in those cases the exception is only partial.

In dealings with its own potential enemies and with ongoing wars, governments similarly substitute symbols for accomplishment. A "detente" with Russia turns out to mean no letup in the arms race, or in the frequent shooting wars in which America and Russia support opposing sides, or in periodic confrontations of other kinds. In short, the era of detente is indistinguishable from the era of cold and hot war so far as military competition and the threat of war are concerned. What detente does mean is political gesturing between the White House and the Kremlin that serves the domestic political interests of both leaders but is insulated from their military policy moves. The White House for a time became Brezhnev's ally in resisting congressional pressure to intervene in behalf of Soviet Jews, while, in 1974, Brezhnev helped Nixon's pretense of foreign policy accomplishments as a ploy in fighting off Watergate investigations.

This tactic is viable in the degree that people feel threatened by international developments; for their fears, together with their powerlessness as individuals to deal with international problems, lead them to welcome displays of strong leadership. In this way anxiety focuses public hopes on personalities and permits leaders to maintain power through a dramaturgy of coping, regardless of results, which always look ambiguous and provisional in any case. This psychological process explains why every regime both encourages public anxiety and placates it through rhetoric and reassuring gestures. Americans and Russians are constantly told that the other is ahead in this or that weapons system or that some trouble spot threatens peace or national interests. At the same time both regimes reassure their people that military power and the incumbent leadership are effective. Anxiety and reassurance furnish a supportive following.

Inflation is another major public problem for which governments offer reassuring rhetoric and gestures more consistently than they provide effective action. The range of gestures on this front between 1971 and 1975 were instructive about the possibilities of maintaining public support while failing: a wage–price freeze from which major industries quickly won exceptions; a series of "phases" that aroused intense discussion and debate, seemingly in direct proportion to the price rises that followed them; high interest rates and tight money; appeals to unions and businessmen to exercise restraint; and "summit" meetings of eminent economists and representatives of interest groups. During the years these policies were most loudly publicized, inflation grew much worse, in part due to other governmental policies defined as serving a wholly different purpose, such as ensuring an adequate supply of oil; but the publicity for periodic new policies undeniably kept protest moderate.

Repeated reminders that inflation is a worldwide problem, therefore allegedly beyond the control of any national government, have also moderated protests, despite steep price increases. The claim that inflation elsewhere in the world exonerates governmental regimes is still another instance of the structuring of a social problem so as to cloud perception of who is responsible. Price increases are neither acts of God nor an infection by microorganisms, though those are the implicit metaphors in the "worldwide problem" defense. They are acts of sellers of goods and servcies, and they increase the profits of many firms substantially. If businessmen, especially multinational corporations, can use the fact of worldwide inflation to justify price rises and win governmental support for these in each country in which they operate, they do so. While the responsibility lies with particular corporations and with governments that permit or encourage their actions, people are easily cued to see the malady as inevitable or as caused by consumers who eat too much or by workers who want a higher standard of living.

Other governmental measures, ostensibly designed to protect the consumer, have long since been shown to yield more in symbolic reassurance and mystification than in protection. Regulatory agencies and public utility commissions serve largely to place a governmental sanction on rate increases that would otherwise be much more militantly resented and resisted. Antitrust laws similarly sanction mergers and pricing agreements, with occasional token wrist slaps to keep the symbolism pure. Such laws have performed these dubious functions for almost a century, and critics and scholars have exposed the hiatus between promise and performance for almost as long. Yet liberals and consumer advocates can be counted on to call for strengthening them whenever their ineffectiveness becomes blatantly apparent, a tactic Thurman Arnold exposed as futile in *The Folklore of Capitalism*, published in 1937. Regulatory commissions continue to serve as symbols of governmental protection of the consumer rather than as evidence that ineffective policies can win public support if people are cued to see them as benevolent. Perhaps the most potent cueing comes from evoking the perception that specific officials, such as members of regulatory boards, are consumer advocates. Once this is done, their actions, their failures to act, and the demonstrably counterproductive results of their policies all fade into something close to invisibility before the symbol of public protection of the economically weak.

Unemployment ranging between 5 and 10 percent of the labor force for many years is accepted, with few political repercussions. In Britain and many other countries a 3 percent unemployment level has been regarded as alarming, suggesting that the level of acceptability is socially cued and that it has little bearing on the extent of actual suffering.

Such developments and their rationalizations are accepted by people who want to believe that they can trust their public officials. The woes of a family whose breadwinner cannot find work are in a different universe of discourse from the unemployment statistics: personal or neighborhood knowledge rather than "public affairs," and the two universes coexist without disturbing each other. Except in the rare instances—such as the mid-thirties—that unemployment becomes a major concern and the government portrays it as one, unwelcome facts succumb readily to reassuring cues.

Welfare and crime programs that fail also regularly evoke public demands for more of the same policies. In these areas the depiction of public authorities and professionals as effective and benevolent is complemented with the depiction of the poor as pathological: lazy, inadequate, sick, or inherently motivated to commit crimes ("hard core"). As a result the transmutation of welfare, crime, and similar problems into perceptions of the level of merit of individuals achieves double-barreled power. Competent authorities coping with problems caused by the incompetent, sick, or dangerous multitudes who suffer from them is a more vivid perception than an economic system that produces high unemployment levels, low pay, demeaning and stultifying work, and other pathologies. Legislation requiring welfare recipients to work engenders the belief that laziness is at the heart of the welfare problem and that jobs are plentiful. Longer sentences for theft or for drug violations than for embezzlement, price fixing, or alcoholism reinforce the belief that the poor are prone to crime and irresponsibility while the prosperous, with a few regrettable exceptions, are law abiding, responsible, and respectable. The catalogue of subtle devices through which we authoritatively disseminate and reinforce the conventional beliefs is long. The consequence is that every new alarm about the problems of crime or poverty brings new demands for tougher police measures and more stringent enforcement of the eligibility conditions of welfare legislation.

Watergate, the Pentagon Papers, and revelations of the deception of Congress by officials of the executive branch and by intelligence agencies have made us sensitive to lying in high places. But the more dangerous public misperceptions are of a different sort: much harder to recognize and expose, typically perpetrated in good faith by those who benefit from them, and usually supported by those they deprive.

We all need reassurance that the tremendous power of governments to make our lives contented or miserable is being wielded with integrity, even though we find it impossible or hopelessly wasteful to determine the actual impact of every public policy for ourselves.

In the years since 1965, support for political institutions and incumbents has declined markedly, but this distrust is clearly ambivalent and highly compartmentalized in its effects on behavior. It did not prevent the White House from continuing to wage the Southeast Asian war for at least five years after most of the public began to see it as unnecessary and harmful. Nor did it prevent Nixon's landslide reelection at a time when his personal popularity was low and many who voted for him distrusted him. Rather than imposing constraints on officials, the ambivalence of their constituents often permits continuation of the policies that engender the ambivalence. Popular distrust of the effectiveness of antitrust, public utility, criminal, and welfare laws and of disarmament agreements has always coexisted with the belief that they do minimize transgressions; but these forms of governmental action persist indefinitely, periodically reinforced by demands for their more stringent enforcement, precisely when their ineffectiveness is most apparent.

Just as Lévi-Strauss has recognized that folk myths express "unwelcome contradictions" that help people to live with uncertainty and ambivalence, so contradictory perceptions of ambiguous public issues serve the same purpose. We concomitantly accept the reassuring explanations of authorities and recognize that the reassurance is often unwarranted, even exploitative. But the official explanations are bound to be dominant, for these political beliefs permit people to live with their political worlds and with themselves with a minimum of strain. The alternative means a politicized life of active protest and resistance, and few want it.

There is a related reason people normally accept the conventional explanation in spite of periodic doubts. To accept a belief about serious public issues, whether or not it is a myth, is to define one's own identity. The overwhelming majority want to believe that their own roles are meaningful contributions to a greater good, and so have good reason to accept the reassuring perspective on public affairs, rather than one that upsets both their belief in institutions they have supported and their belief in themselves. To accept contradictory myths is to play the role society demands while at the same time maintaining a measure of personal integrity by recognizing facts inconsistent with the role. In this sense, people survive by occupying coexisting "realities" that only rarely disturb each other.

Individual political leaders evoke praise, blame, enthusiasm, distrust, or hero worship. Sometimes they are charismatic and sometimes they are perceived as embodiments of evil. People tend to incorporate their emotional reactions to developments in their perceptions of leaders, reacting to the presence or absence of peace and of prosperity in terms of likes or dislikes for incumbent officials. Here is a ready outlet for inability to analyze complicated issues and distaste for trying. As a result, leaders may be displaced as a reaction to strong aversion for their policies, but the policies themselves need not be displaced. It is, in fact, the political function of public officials to attract blame or praise; but the link between such emotional outbursts and the choice of public policies is precisely that the catharsis of praising or ousting a leader can readily divert demands for abandoning the policies that failed or divert attention from the many unpublicized lives and careers that are often stunted by actions that symbolize leadership.

The implications of the ability of contemporary governments to maintain support for policies that deny the great majority the values they cherish are evident enough. Though regimes need not be responsive to the large majority of voters, they must respond to the holders of wealth, for without this support elections are lost and key public programs are easily turned into obvious failures rather than ambiguous successes. Compounding the intimate linkage between political and economic elites is the increasing dependence of business profits on public contracts, subsidies, and tax favors. Government grows increasingly responsive to the concentrations of wealth it creates because it does not have to be responsive to the middle class, the working class, or the poor. As this trend continues, industry can also afford insensitivity to customers, workers, and small stockholders.

The consequence is a decline in the quality of life, springing from a lowering of real income; a decrease in the creation of public goods; more stringent identification and regulation of the poor, the wayward, and the unconventional; and more ready resort to cold and hot wars. While these deprivations are bitterly resented, the symbolism of government usually channels the resentment to the wrong targets.

The Stultification of the Individual

Dubious political categorizations cripple individuals directly as well, and are even more destructive of human potentialities than misconceived public policies are. Governments either call directly for individual sacrifice to promote the public interest or they evoke a metaphor of "balance" between the individual's interests and those of society. The term "balance" has no objective meaning in this context, for there is manifestly no scale or reference mark that assures people with opposing interests that an equilibrium has been reached in the way that a butcher's scale satisfies both the seller and the buyer that a quantity of meat weighs a pound. In politics, references to a "balance" are common because they help win general acceptance for the values of those who use the term. This is an appeal for support, not a form of measurement, though its users are likely to deceive themselves as well as others into believing that they are being objective. The use of the term "balance" in political and legal rhetoric exemplifies a categorization that makes an effective appeal because it presents itself as descriptive rather than polemical. It is another instance of governmental language that is preeminently a means of inducing acquiescence in deprivation and of stilling the qualms of those who benefit.

In this century, the "helping professions" have reinforced inequality by equating adjustment to existing social, economic, and political institutions with psychological health. People who do not fit easily into the economic, sexual, social, or military roles expected of them or who seriously question existing institutions are not taken seriously on their own terms, but defined as deviant and in need of rehabilitation, by force if necessary.

Governments have always had to rely on "nonpolitical" symbols to reinforce restrictions of individual autonomy: an afterlife that would reward faith and loyalty and punish heresy, a vision of a future utopia or of a past fall from grace.

In an age of technological achievement it is the symbol of science that works. A call for the "adjusted" individual rationalizes the most repressive stultification of the human spirit, for in learning to conform, people are taught to see themselves as undergoing a cure; and if they have doubts, their counselors, doctors, and trainers reassure them that they will indeed benefit from rehabilitation.

Many people do experience severe suffering, stress, desperation, and bewilderment. Help and support are necessary. But personal dilemmas are not "deviance" unless authorities call them that. The labeling of deviance wins popular support for controls that are the negation of support and help.

Individuality is always a threat to the comfortable, not least because it is contagious. An emphasis on adjustment of the individual to society constricts the wealthy and the powerful as well as the poor and powerless, though the psychological cages of the affluent are more comfortable. They enjoy their creature comforts and their political dominance only as long as they conform to *their* institutional roles. To establish adjustment, rather than fulfillment, as the highest good is to assure a life for everyone that fails to achieve its potentialities.

In the face of the intermeshing symbols that shape dominant political beliefs and perceptions, it is hard to recognize that every proposition that pits an individual's interests against those of society poses a false issue. The individual person exists, and his or her well-being is the point of existence. "Society," "the national interest," and similar terms do not refer to anything that exists. They are symbols that induce people to acquiesce in deprivations of many kinds. They have no consistent meaning any more than they have an existence, for every group sees its own political interests as "the public interest" and demands that others support them for the sake of "society." Employers perceive wage restraint by workers as in the public interest, while consumers see low prices and low profits in the same light. Proponents of a war see the willingness of soldiers to sacrifice their lives in battle as in the public interest, while pacifists see refusal to do so in the same light. Anyone who speaks of balancing individual against common interests or of sacrificing the first for the second is demanding that his or her values be accepted as paramount. But because everyone is socialized to respond positively to "society," "the national interest," and similar condensation symbols, these terms help engender mass acquiescence in material sacrifices, constricted roles, political weakness, existing power hier-archies, and unfulfilled lives.

The result is the stultification of human potentialities rather than their fulfillment: degradation of people into bundles of skills and patterns of inhibition that fit the concern of industry for docile and productive labor, of the state for an uncritical and compliant citi-zenry, of the army for soldiers conditioned to obey and to die on command, and, in some countries, of the church for worshipers ready to sacrifice their material comforts. Through their diverse myths and symbols, these institutions complement one another and reinforce one another's powers to convert human beings into objects with specialized talents that fit into the great hierarchies.

The very gift for self-education, self-discipline, and artistic ex-pression becomes a means for inducing people to sacrifice their lives and their talents for mystical or mythical objectives:

> And how can man die better
> Than by facing fearful odds
> For the ashes of his fathers
> And the temples of his gods?

or

> Ask not what your country can do for you;
> Ask what you can do for your country.

The poetry and the eloquence are in a different world of discourse from analysis of who benefit from sacrifices in the name of fathers' ashes, temples, or country. Some may choose to make the sacrifices in any case and have every right to do so. The point is that symbol-ism presents the choice in terms of a false issue: as though it involved placing the good of the community against private, selfish interests, when the choice is always between one group and another, with the group benefiting from mystical appeals always a relatively small and privileged one.

The grand, conspicuous symbols are potent only because thou-sands of subtle, unrecognized symbols embedded in everyday polit-ical language and gestures do the real work of evoking beliefs and perceptions, as my earlier chapters try to show. The continuous evocation of problematic beliefs through categorizations and figures of speech that are not recognized as symbolic at all makes terms like "society" and "the national interest" look like calls to a higher duty rather than public relations ploys. The important and the difficult task for political analysts is to identify the consequences of subtle symbolism, for it is the foundation of political power and of political illusion. It induces the great mass of people in every land and in every era to live much of their lives bemused by a mythical past, preparing for a mythical future, creating mythical heroes and devils, and sacrificing their wholeness as individuals to support inequalities in wealth and power that impoverish even those who have the most of them.

In these circumstances "deviance" is inevitable. Often it is a signal of rejection of constricting institutions, a form of self-assertion that can reasonably be defined as healthy rather than as pathological. To brush away the prevailing symbolism completely is probably impossible, but the effort is necessary and some success is obviously feasible.

Neither individual suffering nor an offense against law or morality is evidence that the "deviant" must be forced to conform or be isolated from the great majority so bemused by political symbols that they adjust uncomplainingly to their assigned roles. Every case of these pathologies is added proof that economic and social institutions need to be adjusted to the needs of human beings.

Index

Institute for Research on Poverty
Monograph Series

In Preparation